BOOKKEEPING TAX & BUSINESS WORKBOOK

FOR THE SELF-EMPLOYED - 2022/2023

Elyse V.K Burns-Hill

AMAZON BEST-SELLING AUTHOR

 **Brilliant book all Avon Reps should own one!**

ISBN: 9798827431879

Edition 1 Published November 2023

Printed By Amazon Publishing Services in the UK

Published by Prosperity Publishing
c/o ElyseBH Consulting Ltd
Hursley Park Road
Winchester
Hampshire
SO21 2JN

Table of Contents

About the Author

Elyse Burns-Hill

Elyse qualified with the Association of Chartered Certified Accountants (ACCA) and is a practising accountant supervised by the Institute of Financial Accountants. She started her Accountancy career at PwC in Malta in 2010 and has also practised in firms in Jersey, Channel Islands and Hampshire, UK.

In 2020, just six months after joining forces with another accountant to run an accountancy firm, he passed away, leaving Elyse to manage the company and all the clients by herself. She was thrown into being an employer, being the sole contact for over 100 clients and supporting all those clients remotely and through the Covid pandemic.

Luckily, Elyse's background in business systems, IT, sales and marketing, along with her years of experience in accountancy, allowed her to flourish and learn a vast amount about herself and business in a very short time.

Elyse is a best-selling author, having achieved best-seller status on Amazon with two of the previous incarnations of this book. She has published multiple titles and is publishing more books every year. Elyse has always loved reading books, but when she ran out of stories to read at the school library at the age of 15, she started writing her own. As an adult, she has the bug for writing and publishing books, mainly non-fiction, but she does have a sneaky plan to return to fiction very soon...watch this space.

Elyse lives in Hampshire with her two beautiful daughters, and the family is currently awaiting the arrival of two feline babies. She loves adventures in nature and shares her escapades on Instagram. You can also find her on YouTube, Facebook and LinkedIn, talking passionately about business to whomever will listen!

Preface

While plenty of people know that they need to do something about tax returns, there are just as many people who don't know anything about tax returns.

I came to realise it when, after signing up to be an AVON Rep after the birth of my first daughter, I saw all these questions in the AVON Rep Facebook groups asking questions about tax, and some reps, absolutely horrified, realised that they should have been submitting tax returns for the last few years they'd been running an AVON business.

I've lost count of the number of phone calls I've taken from reps telling me they feel sick to the core with fright that HMRC will pin them down and fine the pants off them for not submitting their tax returns on time.

I started a Facebook group for Avon Reps to help them understand their duties and how, practically, to keep all their records and submit their own tax return.

That group evolved into the first version of this book, which I printed from my home printer, bought a wire binding machine, bound, and posted out to reps.

The book proved popular (even though I'm thoroughly embarrassed about that first version of the book now, with a few typos and unfinished sentences!), so in the next tax year, I issued a new, updated version of it – and I published it to Amazon so that I didn't have to print, bind and post every single copy.

For the next few tax years, there was an iteration and improvement each year, until this year, when I gave the book a massive overhaul, re-wrote large parts of it, added a considerable amount of content, and re-designed it to be helpful to all sole traders rather than just AVON Reps.

So this book results from that constant iteration and evolution over the last few years. The story of how this book came into being is a business lesson in itself – the first version of anything you do might be a little embarrassing. The very first version of Apple's iPhone was quite embarrassing compared to what they are releasing now.

Every business with a first-class product will go through that evolutionary stage – as the business owner; you must have the patience and fortitude to keep going, re-hashing, and re-iterating. Eventually, you come out with something quite remarkable. I'm proud of how far my book has come, but I think I can do better, and can legitimately call it remarkable in the not-too-distant future!

I hope you find this book helpful, and I'm always happy to hear feedback so that my next iteration can be even better!

Chapter 1: Using This Book

Welcome to a journey of financial empowerment and clarity. This book is designed to be your companion, guide, and workbook as you navigate the nuances of managing finances and taxes for your business. Whether you're a seasoned sole trader or just starting, the path to understanding financial matters needn't be solitary or stressful. Here, we present a flexible approach to learning infused with opportunities to practice, reflect, and even unwind.

Flexible Reading Approach
You can read this book from cover to cover, immersing yourself in a comprehensive understanding of small business finances. Alternatively, feel free to dip in and out, using it as a reference for specific topics as they become relevant to your journey. Each chapter stands alone, offering deep insights into bookkeeping, tax and business.

Teach to Learn
As you absorb the information within these pages, consider the power of teaching as a learning tool. Studies show that when we read with the intention to teach, we understand and retain information more effectively. Share your newfound knowledge with a partner, a friend, or even your children. Articulate what you've learned; it will reinforce your understanding and confidence.

Interactive Workbook
Throughout this book, you'll find exercises designed to apply the concepts to your own business. Spaces provided within the text will allow you to write down thoughts, work through calculations, and reflect on how the information pertains to your specific situation. These exercises are crucial for cementing your understanding, so don't skip them!

Mindfulness and Stress Reduction
Taxation and financial planning can be overwhelming, hence why we've sprinkled several mindfulness colouring pages throughout the book. These are meant to offer you a respite from the numbers and a moment to reduce stress. Take advantage of these pages to clear your mind and return to the numbers refreshed.

Community Support
Use the accompanying Facebook group to ask questions, share insights, or seek clarification. This community is an extension of the book, offering you support and collective wisdom from fellow sole traders and financial experts.

Designed for Ease
My aim is to demystify the complexities of financial management and make it as accessible as possible. We understand that everyone's financial literacy journey is different, and we've strived to make this book as clear and user-friendly as possible. However, your feedback is invaluable. If there's something you don't understand or think could be explained better, please reach out.

Conclusion

This book is more than just a source of information; it's a tool for action, a medium for learning, and a catalyst for personal business growth. By engaging with the content actively, you will be taking significant steps toward financial proficiency and peace of mind. So, let's begin this journey with an open mind, a willingness to learn, and a commitment to apply these lessons to the real world.

Chapter 2: The Big Questions

Have you ever had a nagging question about your business paperwork and didn't know where to find the answer? Let's take a stroll through some of the most common queries sole traders have. And remember, if your specific question isn't here, feel free to join our friendly Facebook group to chat with other entrepreneurs like you!

What records should I keep for my business?

You know, it's not as complicated as you might think. Essentially, you'll want to hold onto anything that supports the figures you'll be sharing with HMRC. As we dive deeper into the book, you'll get more familiar with these specifics. For now, hang onto anything that seems important.

Documents to treasure include:
- Sales invoices from your services or products
- Order forms if you're selling products
- Bank statements (ideally from an account you use solely for your business - more on that later in this chapter)
- Receipts and purchase invoices for any business-related purchases.

Do I send all these records to HMRC?

No, you don't need to submit any of your records. You complete the Self-Assessment form with the calculated numbers and submit that. If HMRC ever wants to review your documents to check that your Self-Assessment was accurate, they will contact you and arrange to view your records. (It's unlikely that will happen, but you must be ready just in case).

How long should I keep these records?

Here's a simple rule of thumb: Retain your records for five years from the tax year's deadline. For instance, documents supporting the 22/23 tax return should be cherished until January 2029. Time flies, right?

Why register with HMRC?

Being self-employed or a sole trader brings certain responsibilities, including keeping HMRC informed about your earnings. It ensures everything's above board and you're taxed accurately.

If your annual sales fall below £1000, things can be different (let's unravel that next).

If my earnings are less than £1000, do I still need to submit a return?

This one's a bit intricate, but let's break it down. The £1000 threshold relates to turnover, not profit. To put it in perspective, selling £83 of products or services every month gets you close to this limit - £83 x 12 months = £990.

Under this amount? You might not need self-assessment. However, there can be exceptions:
Suppose you are already registered but still qualify for the allowance. In that case, you can use it on your self-assessment INSTEAD of claiming your business expenses. You will still need to keep records showing your turnover, i.e., all your order forms and other receipts from eBay or markets.

If you are employed and sell to your employer, you disqualify yourself from claiming the allowance. Colleagues are ok, but not your boss.

The £1000 allowance applies to all your self-employed income. So, for example, if you're an AVON rep and you also run a childminding business, you still only get the single £1000 allowance.

If you qualify for the allowance but look like you will make a loss for the year with your income less than all your claimable expenses, you might be better off registering the loss to offset it against future profits rather than claiming the allowance.

If you want to be able to pay class 2 NI contributions, you will need to register and submit the self-assessment.

If you want to claim Tax-Free Childcare for childcare costs based on your self-employment income, you must register and submit the self-assessment.

If you want to claim Maternity Allowance based on your self-employment income, you must register and submit the self-assessment.

The nuances can be many, so if in doubt, here's a handy link - https://www.gov.uk/guidance/tax-free-allowances-on-property-and-trading-income#trade to government information to clarify things further.

When do I register as Self-Employed with HMRC?

You must register with HMRC no later than 5 October in your business's second tax year; otherwise, HMRC *may* apply penalties to your account.

So, what does that mean?

If you started your business between 6 April 2021 and 5 April 2022, you would need to have registered by 5 October 2022.

However, I would advise you not to leave it to the last minute to register; do it as soon as possible.

How do I register as Self-Employed with HMRC?

The easiest way to register for Self-Employment is to use the online form:
https://www.gov.uk/log-in-file-self-assessment-tax-return/register-if-youre-self-employed

When you register, you will:

- create a government gateway login (make sure you keep a note of your login – it's easy to forget as you only use it once a year!)

- get a letter with your 10-digit Unique Taxpayer Reference (UTR)

- be enrolled for the Self-Assessment online service; once you have activated the service using the activation code, you will receive by letter within ten days of registration. Once you receive it, you'll need to login to your Government Gateway as soon as possible, so that you can type in the activation code. The activation code expires in 30 days, so do it as soon as you can.

I've missed the registration deadline! What do I do?

Give HMRC a call.

They are generally not a problem if you go to them and say you didn't realise you had to register, you bought a book or joined a group on Facebook and found out that you should have been registered, and you've given them a call straight away.

Don't take that as gospel, but if THEY find that you've been running a business without registering, they will likely impose penalties.

If you self-declare that you should have been registered but weren't, you will get into less trouble!

They will probably ask you when you started your business (so make sure you have that date ready) and ask you to complete the missed returns since that date.

What is Payment on Account?

Oh, you've hit upon one of those nifty terms that might sound a tad confusing, but let's break it down together!

Imagine you're in a restaurant, and they ask you to pay a deposit in advance for a large group booking. This deposit is kind of a guarantee or a head-start on the final bill. Well, 'Payment on Account' works similarly but for your taxes.

HMRC sometimes asks self-employed folks and sole traders to pay their next year's tax bill in advance based on the current year's earnings. This happens in two instalments. The idea is to help spread out the tax payment and give HMRC some assurance.

Now, why would they ask this of you? If your Self-Assessment tax bill is above £1000 and you're paying less than 80% of all the tax you owe through PAYE, you'll be asked to make these payments.

These payments pop up twice a year:
1. **31st January** - This is the same day you pay your previous year's balance.
2. **31st July** - A mid-year top-up of sorts.

Keep in mind, though, if you end up overpaying because your income was lower than expected, HMRC will owe you a refund. On the other hand, if your income was higher, you'd owe a little extra.

Does it sound a bit daunting? Don't fret. Just keep track of your earnings, HMRC will let you know if and when you will need to start making these payments. It is worth preparing your tax return as early as possible though if you leave it till the last minute in January to file your return, and then you find out you have to make a payment on account for the first time, it might make finding the cash to pay 150% of your tax bill a little more difficult.

It does feel like an unfair sting in the first year you have to make this payment on account, but when you cease being a sole trader, you appreciate why they do it. Finding the extra cash for an entire year of tax bill when you have stopped running that business can be difficult, where you've been paying on account, it means when you stop your business, your tax bills are more or less all paid up.

How much tax do I have to pay?

Ah, the million-pound question – or hopefully not quite that much! But seriously, understanding how much tax you owe is crucial, so let's break it down together.

First off, remember, being self-employed or a sole trader doesn't mean you're taxed at a different rate than employees. Instead, what differs is how and when you pay it.

Your tax is based on your **profits**, not your total income. Let's dive into the simple formula:

Total Income (what you've earned from your products, services, or any other sources)
minus **Business Expenses** (all those allowable costs involved in running your business)
= **Profit** (the magic number on which you're taxed)

Now, based on this profit:

1. **Personal Allowance:** For most people, there's a certain amount you can earn each year without paying tax, known as your personal allowance. For the 22/23 Tax Year, the personal allowance is £12,570. This is reviewed every year by the government, but it has remained at this level for the last few years now.

2. **Basic Rate:** Profits that fall above the personal allowance and up to £50,270 (for 22/23) are taxed at 20%.

3. **Higher Rate:** Profits between £50,271 and £150,000 are taxed at 40%.

4. **Additional Rate:** Anything above £150,000 gets taxed at a cool 45%.

But wait, there's a twist! Sole traders also have to consider National Insurance Contributions (NICs). There are two main classes for sole traders:

- Class 2 NIC: A flat weekly rate if your profits are above a certain threshold.
- Class 4 NIC: A percentage of your profits, applied when you earn above another threshold.

It sounds like a jigsaw puzzle, doesn't it? But with a dash of organisation, maybe a sprinkle of professional guidance through the Facebook Group, and a pinch of perseverance, you'll get a clear picture of your tax dues in no time.

If you're ever in doubt, HMRC has some useful online tools, and calculators to help, or, of course, pop that question into our Facebook group – we're all in this together!

What is Voluntary National Insurance?

When we talk about National Insurance (NI), we're usually referring to the mandatory contributions that employees, employers, and the self-employed make to qualify for certain state benefits, such as the State Pension. But sometimes, life throws curveballs, and there might be gaps in your National Insurance record. This is where Voluntary National Insurance steps into the spotlight.

So, why would anyone pay NI voluntarily? Good question! Here are a couple of reasons:

1. **State Pension:** To qualify for the full State Pension, you need a certain number of qualifying years on your National Insurance record. If you have gaps (maybe you took time out of work or earned below the threshold), making voluntary contributions can help you fill in those blanks.

2. **Benefits & Allowances:** Apart from the pension, having a complete NI record ensures you're eligible for other benefits like Jobseeker's Allowance or Maternity Allowance.

How do you make these voluntary contributions? There are two classes to consider:

- Class 2: If you were self-employed but had low earnings or weren't trading for a part of the year.
- Class 3: If you were either not working or lived abroad, among other reasons.

The rates for these classes differ, and it's essential to check which one applies to your situation.

Now, before you dash off to top up, pause and think: Is it worth it? It's a good idea to seek advice or use online tools to see if making these payments will indeed benefit you in the long run. Remember, it's all about getting the most bang for your buck!

If you're ever in a muddle about this, don't hesitate to drop a line in our Facebook group. After all, sharing is caring, and many heads are often better than one!

We've talked about taxing profits, but what happens if my business made a loss?

We've all heard the saying, "Every cloud has a silver lining." In the world of sole trading, that silver lining might be the way we can handle business losses. Now, I know the term "business losses" sounds daunting – kind of like spilling coffee on a pristine white shirt. But fret not! Let's demystify what business losses are and how you can approach them in a way that might even benefit your tax situation

Understanding Business Losses:

Simply put, a business loss occurs when your allowable business expenses exceed your business income in a tax year. So, if you spent more on your business (on things like supplies, marketing, or other costs) than you earned, you're looking at a loss.

So, what can you do with this loss?

1. Offset Against Other Income: One of the most common ways to use a business loss is to offset it against other sources of income you might have in the same tax year. This could be salary from another job, rental income, or other types of taxable income. This means you'd pay less tax for that year. Sounds good, right?

2. Carry It Backwards: Imagine having a time machine where you could travel back to a previous tax year (but please, leave the dinosaurs alone). You can carry back your loss to offset against profits you made in earlier years, potentially resulting in a tax refund.

3. Carry It Forward: Maybe you're feeling optimistic about next year (and you should!). In this case, you can carry forward the loss and offset it against future profits from your business. This option is especially useful if you expect higher profits in the upcoming years.

What should you consider?

- **Keep Thorough Records:** Just as you'd cherish photographs of memorable moments, ensure you have clear records of all your business transactions. If you claim a loss on your tax return, you'll need evidence to support it.

- **Consult a Professional**: Every sole trader's situation is unique. If you're unsure about the best way to handle a loss, a chat with an accountant or financial advisor can be invaluable. Think of it as asking a friend for their favourite book recommendation – tailored advice just for you.

Remember:

While no one starts a business expecting to make a loss, it's a natural part of the entrepreneurial journey, especially in the early stages or during challenging times. The key is understanding how to handle it and finding that silver lining.

Stay resilient, and remember that losses can provide learning opportunities and potential tax reliefs. You've got this!

Do I need to be VAT registered, and how does it work?

Ah, VAT! Another one of those acronyms that can make a sole trader's head spin, right?

VAT stands for *Value Added Tax*. Think of it as a consumption tax that's added to the price of most goods and services. But, as a business owner, you have some responsibilities tied to it.

Let's break this question down into sub-questions and look at them one at a time:

1. Do I need to register?

You only need to register for VAT if:

- Your VAT taxable turnover (i.e., the total of everything you sell that isn't VAT exempt) is more than the current threshold in a 12-month period. As of the publication date, the threshold was £85,000, but always make sure to check the current figure on the HMRC website, as it can change.

- You believe your turnover will exceed this threshold in the next 30-day period.

Note: Even if you don't hit the threshold, you can voluntarily register for VAT. Why? Read on!

2. How does VAT registration benefit me?

Claiming Back: Once registered, you can start reclaiming VAT on your business-related purchases. This can be a significant saving for *some* businesses.

Business Image: Being VAT registered can give clients and suppliers the impression that your business is larger or more established than it might be.

3. What does being VAT registered entail?

You'll need to add VAT to your sales invoices. The standard rate is currently 20%, but there are reduced rates for some products and services.

Every three months, you'll need to submit a VAT return to HMRC outlining how much VAT you've charged and how much you've paid. If you've charged more than you've paid, you'll owe HMRC the difference. If you've paid more than you've charged, you'll have a nice refund coming your way!

Keep detailed records of all invoices and receipts. There's software out there that can help with this – my favourite is Xero.

4. I've heard about different VAT schemes; what does that mean?

There are various VAT schemes available, such as the Flat Rate Scheme, which might be more advantageous depending on your business. It's worth looking into these or seeking advice to see which might be the best fit.

5. How do I register?

You can register online on the HMRC website. Once you're registered, you'll receive a VAT registration certificate with your VAT number, the date of your first VAT return, and the payment deadline.

A word of caution – there are tax professionals who specialise just in VAT; it's a whole other animal compared to self-assessment. If you do feel you want to or if you need to register for VAT, you would do yourself a service to have a meeting with an accountant to ensure you are getting things set up correctly. The rules are stricter for VAT, so you do want to make sure you are doing it right.

What's the difference between 'cash basis' and 'traditional accounting'?

Imagine your business as a ship sailing the vast ocean of entrepreneurship. Both 'cash basis' and 'traditional accounting' (often referred to as 'accrual accounting') are like different navigation tools to chart your financial journey. Each has its merits, and the one you choose depends on how you prefer to plot your course.

1. Cash Basis Accounting:

Think of this as the "what you see is what you get" method.

How it Works: You only record income when it lands in your bank account and expenses when they leave your account. Simple, right? So if a customer buys from you in February but pays in March, you'd record that sale in March.

Pros: It's super straightforward, making it a popular choice for smaller businesses or sole traders. You always know where you stand, as you're only dealing with real cash in and out.

Cons: It doesn't give a complete picture if there are time lags between when you earn income or incur an expense and when the cash actually changes hands.

2. Traditional (Accrual) Accounting:

This method is like having a crystal ball that lets you glimpse both the present and the future of your finances.

How it Works: Income and expenses are recorded when they are earned or incurred, regardless of when the money changes hands. So, if you invoiced a client in February, even if they paid you in April, you'd record that income in February.

Pros: It provides a more comprehensive overview of your financial position, as it includes pending payments and upcoming bills. This makes it ideal for larger businesses or those with complex financial situations.

Cons: It's a bit more complicated than cash basis accounting, and you might find yourself keeping an eye on those outstanding invoices a bit more closely!

So, which should you choose?

If you're a sole trader with a straightforward financial situation, the 'cash basis' method might be right up your alley. It's simpler and less time-consuming. However, if your business is growing, has inventory, or deals with credit terms, then 'traditional accounting' can offer a clearer overall picture.

Regardless of which method feels right for your business, the key is consistency. Once you pick a method, stick to it. And remember, if you're ever in doubt or need some guidance, our ever-helpful Facebook group is here to help. After all, navigating the world of accounting is always easier with some fellow sailors by your side!

Should I set up a separate business bank account?

Picture this: you're making a scrumptious salad. You've got your crisp lettuce, juicy tomatoes, crunchy cucumbers, and...wait, is that a sneaky gummy bear hiding among the greens? Just like that salad, mixing business and personal finances can make things, well, a bit messy. But is a separate business bank account the right choice for everyone? Let's dissect the pros and cons to help you make an informed decision.

Why you might want a separate business bank account:

1. Crystal Clear Finances: Just as you'd separate your recyclables from non-recyclables, having a dedicated business account makes it easier to see what's coming in and going out of your business. It'll be a breeze come tax time or when you're reviewing your finances.

2. Professionalism: When clients or customers see payments addressed to or from a business-named account, it can add an extra layer of professionalism. Plus, it feels pretty cool, doesn't it?

3. Avoiding Mix-Ups: It's easy to mistakenly record a personal expense as a business one or vice versa when everything's in one pot. Separate accounts can help you sidestep these slip-ups.

Why you might stick with your personal bank account for now:

1. Simplicity: If you're just testing the waters with a new venture or your business transactions are minimal, managing one account might feel more straightforward.

2. Costs: Business bank accounts sometimes come with fees or minimum balance requirements. It's essential to weigh the costs against the benefits.

3. Transfer Delays: Transferring money between personal and business accounts might not always be instantaneous, which could be inconvenient in certain situations.

So, what's the verdict?

If your business transactions are ramping up, or if you're finding it challenging to distinguish between personal and business finances, it's probably a good time to consider setting up a dedicated business bank account. However, if you're running a smaller operation or just starting, and you feel comfortable tracking business expenses in your personal account, you might hold off for a while.

It is also worth remembering that once your business gets to a certain level of self-employed income, it might get the bank's attention – they have to follow slightly stricter rules for accounts with business income and expenses in, so they won't be happy to continue letting you use your personal account. I've heard stories of people who have had their banks tell them they need to open a new account for their business, but I've not spoken to someone yet who has. You should be fine while your business is small, but once it starts to get bigger, make sure you give this some thought.

Always remember, no decision is set in stone. As your business evolves, so too can your approach to managing its finances. And if ever in doubt, seeking advice from a financial professional or our supportive Facebook community can provide clarity.

What kind of insurance do I need for my business?

Not technically a tax question, but it is something I'm asked a lot.

Every business, whether you're offering products, services, or both, comes with its unique set of risks. Insurance is like that trusty umbrella you pack on a cloudy day—it's there to protect you when unexpected challenges rain down. So, let's break down the most common types of insurance that sole traders often consider:

1. Public Liability Insurance:
Imagine a client tripping over a loose cable in your workspace or a product you've sold causes some unintended damage. This insurance covers any legal fees or compensation claims if a third party (like a client or customer) gets injured or their property is damaged because of your business activities.

2. Professional Indemnity Insurance:
For those of you offering advice or professional services, this one's a biggie. It covers legal costs and expenses if you're accused of providing inadequate advice, services, or designs that cause your client to lose money.

3. Product Liability Insurance:
If you're selling products, listen up! This insurance covers you if a product you've sold causes injury or damage. For instance, if a beauty product you sell causes a skin reaction, this insurance can step in. However, remember that if you are a re-seller of that beauty product, the liability for a skin reaction would fall on the manufacturer, not on you.

4. Employers' Liability Insurance:
If you employ staff, even if it's just one person, it's typically a legal requirement to have this insurance. It covers you if an employee gets injured or falls ill because of the work they do for you.

5. Business Equipment & Contents Insurance:
For all those gadgets, tools, and equipment that help you run your business, this insurance can cover the costs of repairing or replacing them if they get damaged, lost, or stolen.

6. Business Interruption Insurance:
Imagine a flood damaging your workspace, causing you to halt your operations for a few weeks. This insurance covers the loss of income you'd face due to such unexpected interruptions.

7. Personal Accident Insurance:

This one's for you, dear sole trader. If you're injured or fall ill and can't work, this insurance can provide a weekly pay-out, or a lump sum, to keep you afloat.

8. Motor Insurance:

If you use your vehicle for business (other than just commuting), you'll likely need more than standard personal car insurance. Whether it's delivering products or visiting clients, make sure you're covered for business-related trips.

And there we are, a handy guide to business insurance. Remember, the right insurance mix depends on your specific business, its risks, and your personal preferences. Always consider chatting with an insurance broker or advisor to get tailored advice. And of course, if you have more questions, our friendly Facebook group is just a click away. Insurance might not be the most glamorous part of business, but with the right cover, you can sleep a little easier at night!

What happens if I decide to close down or change the structure of my business?

Ah, the ebb and flow of the entrepreneurial journey! Deciding to close down your business or even change its structure isn't an unusual decision. Much like how a ship might need a new course direction or even to drop its anchor for a while, businesses too evolve. Let's dive deep and see what happens when you decide to make such a move.

Closing Down Your Business:

1. Inform HMRC: The first port of call is our friends over at HMRC. Let them know you're no longer trading as a sole trader. They'll provide guidance on any final tax responsibilities you might have.

2. Settle Your Debts: Before you can close shop, ensure that all your business debts are settled. This includes any outstanding invoices, loans, or owed taxes.

3. Dispose of Business Assets: Any assets owned by the business? These can be sold, recycled, or even donated. Remember to keep a record of these transactions as they might have tax implications.

4. Keep Records: Even after shutting down, the captain's log (or in this case, your business records) needs to be kept for about five years. This is in case HMRC decides to look into your affairs in the future.

Changing the Structure of Your Business:

Maybe you're thinking of going from a sole trader to a partnership or even a limited company. It's like upgrading from a canoe to a luxury yacht!

1. Notify HMRC: Again, start by informing HMRC of your intentions. They can give you some guidance on how to transition and any tax implications.

2. Register the New Entity: If you're transitioning to a limited company, for instance, you'll need to register it and get a new company number.

3. Transfer Assets: The assets from your sole trader business will now need to be transferred to the new structure. This might have tax implications, especially if there are gains involved.

4. New Bank Accounts: Depending on the change, you might need new business bank accounts to represent the new entity.

5. Update Your Clients: Just as you'd send postcards from a new destination, inform your clients about the change. It's professional and ensures they know how to engage with your revamped business.

I would highly recommend working with an accountant to transfer your trade to a limited company, they will be able to help you stay compliant and do things in the right order. If you would like some more information on starting a new limited company, I'm just finishing up writing another book – search my name on Amazon and it should come up.

Jot down some of your own questions here, don't forget to write the answers down when you get them too, so you don't forget them!

Q _____
_____
_____

A _____
_____
_____
_____
_____
_____
_____

Q _____
_____
_____

A _____
_____
_____
_____
_____
_____

Q _____
_____
_____

A _____
_____

Q _____

A _____

Q _____

A _____

Chapter 3: Introduction to Bookkeeping

In this chapter, we'll delve into the intricacies of bookkeeping essentials that sole traders should keep an eye on for tax purposes. If you're seeking benefits or grants, these records will also be useful.
To stay organised, consider maintaining a folder where you store all your purchase invoices and related documentation. A systematised approach will pay dividends in the long run!

If you're just stepping into the business realm beyond personal finances, the amount of information might seem overwhelming. However, take things one step at a time, seek answers to your queries, and remember - every successful entrepreneur started somewhere. You've got this!

Bank Account

We have already touched on the bank account in Chapter 2, but here are a few more thoughts.

If you can, get a bank account that is solely dedicated to your sole trader business. It doesn't *have* to be a business bank account as this can often cost you more to run. Although be aware that the banks don't like you using personal accounts for business as they have different rules and compliance requirements, so if they find you using a personal account, they will ask you to set up a business account.

The idea behind this is that it will be easier to keep track of your business transactions but also remind you to keep your business finances separate from your personal finances. So, for example, when you purchase a product that you normally sell for your own personal use, you transfer the cost of that from your personal bank account to your business bank account.

There are loads of online banks that allow you to set up a bank account relatively easily. I've used many of them, for both business and personal accounts, but my favourite (for a personal account) is Monzo. If you plan on using online bookkeeping software such as Xero where you'd like to link the bank feed into the bookkeeping software, don't use Monzo, you'll have to pay for the Pro subscription to get the bank feed capability. The Starling account would work well for that.

If you'd like some more information on different types of bank accounts, have a watch of my video:

www.elyseburns-hill.com/btb23-bankaccounts

Terminology

There are a lot of terminologies involved here, and it does help to have an understanding before continuing. I have simplified it in some areas, as you don't need to know the full accounting definitions to get the right numbers in the right places.

Sales/Turnover/Income – you will see I use these words interchangeably. Basically, it is the amount of money that a business takes.
- Customer orders – what the customer actually paid for their order (after including any loyalty discounts and freebie items etc);
- Sales prices at markets or events;

- Client invoices when you're performing a service for them;
- Commission received from sales you've made where you've sent your customer to the company to transact with directly (if you handle money or product to do with that transaction, you're not receiving commission and should bookkeep the total sale and the total costs).

Cost of Sales – the cost of products or services needed to fulfil the orders/sales that make up your turnover figure

Gross Profit is your turnover minus your cost of sales. The self-assessment tax return doesn't ask for this figure, but you might come across it occasionally. To confirm, gross turnover, is not the same as gross profit, so if you read about gross turnover or gross sales, it is not the same. Sometimes HMRC guidance talks about gross turnover, and some people mistakenly understand it to mean gross profit.

Expenses - the rest of your expenses are things like mileage, work from home, business cards, bank/cc processing costs, postage etc etc) – we'll go into much more depth about what you can claim later in this chapter.

Net Profit is calculated as *Turnover* minus *Cost of Sales* minus *Expenses*. Or you can calculate it as *Gross Profit* minus *Expenses*.
Again, not a figure that your tax return asks for, but it does calculate it for you from the turnover and expense figures. It should match your net profit calculation; if it doesn't, you'll need to figure out why. It is this number that is taxed at the amount appropriate to your circumstances.

Orders and Sales to Customers

Product Based Businesses

For product-based businesses, meticulous documentation of sales activities is indispensable for both operational clarity and regulatory compliance. At the forefront of these documents are sales invoices, which detail the goods sold, their quantities, prices, and the total amounts due. These invoices act as evidence of the sale transaction and typically include the names and addresses of the seller and buyer, date of sale, description of goods sold, and any applicable taxes or discounts.

Additionally, it's imperative to maintain *sales receipts*, which confirm that a payment has been received from a customer. Sales receipts are particularly crucial for point-of-sale transactions, where payment is often made immediately. For businesses that offer terms to their clients, keeping a systematic record of accounts receivable is vital. This log should detail outstanding invoices, their respective due dates, and any follow-ups or payment plans in place.

Lastly, in scenarios where goods are returned or exchanged, having a returns and exchanges log ensures that such transactions are tracked, and any financial adjustments are accounted for. Together, these documents form the backbone of a product-based business's sales record-keeping and provide clarity, accuracy, and accountability in its financial dealings.

For businesses operating on a door-to-door sales model, like AVON, Body Shop at Home, or Usborne Books, there's an additional layer of documentation to consider. Given the direct, in-person nature of transactions, it's crucial to have a comprehensive *order form system*. These forms should capture the customer's details, the date of order, products requested, and the agreed-upon price. It acts as an immediate record of a sale or order commitment and can be invaluable in the event of disputes or clarifications.

Additionally, given that many of these sales may occur on credit with payment expected later, keeping a clear *list of outstanding* amounts from individual customers becomes essential. It ensures timely follow-up and collection. Furthermore, given the potential for returns or exchanges in such a model, always provide customers with a copy of their order or receipt. This not only builds trust but also streamlines any potential return or exchange processes, ensuring that both the business and the customer have a smooth, transparent transaction experience.

Service Based Businesses

For service-based businesses, accurate record-keeping is equally crucial, though the nature of the documentation differs from product-based ventures. Here's what service providers should focus on:

1. Contracts or Service Agreements: Every service provided, especially if it's substantial or extends over a period of time, should be governed by a clear contract or agreement. This document outlines the scope of the service, terms of payment, the duration of engagement, confidentiality clauses, and other essential terms. It acts as a binding commitment between the provider and the client and sets expectations clearly for both parties.

2. Invoices: After the provision of services, or sometimes in advance or during, it's crucial to provide clients with detailed invoices. The invoice should break down the services offered, the rate, any taxes or additional charges, and the total amount. It also sets the payment terms, like due dates, acceptable payment methods, and late fee clauses.

3. Receipts: Upon receiving payment, always provide a receipt, whether digital or physical, as proof of payment. This aids in resolving any future disputes regarding payments and ensures transparency.

4. Timesheets or Logbooks: For businesses that bill by the hour or need to record the time spent on specific tasks (like consultants, designers, or lawyers), maintaining a daily or weekly timesheet is essential. This not only justifies the billed hours to clients but also helps in internal productivity assessments.

5. Feedback and Service Completion Forms: Especially relevant for services where the results might be subjective (like training, counselling, or consultancy), having a form where clients can confirm the receipt and satisfaction of services can be invaluable. This serves as proof of service delivery and can also act as a tool for improving business offerings based on client feedback.

For businesses operating on a door-to-door model offering services (like home cleaning, gardening, or personalised consultancy), it's essential to have a system to document appointments. This can be an appointment book or digital scheduler. Additionally, carrying a booklet of pre-printed service agreement forms can be beneficial. As services are often intangible, providing a tangible record of the agreed-upon service can reassure clients and maintain professionalism. It's also wise to keep a record of any follow-up visits or post-service checks to ensure customer satisfaction and address any concerns promptly.

Don't Get Overwhelmed

Stepping into the world of business, with its myriad tasks and responsibilities, can sometimes feel overwhelming, especially when faced with a list of best practices to follow. While the documentation and processes mentioned above represent an ideal framework for meticulous business management, remember that Rome wasn't built in a day (this is my favourite phrase and one I must remind myself constantly!). It's important to pace yourself.

Not every business will have the resources or the need to implement all these practices from day one. And that's perfectly okay. The key is to prioritise based on your specific business model, clientele, and resources. Start with the essentials that directly affect your operations and customer relations. As your business grows, you can incrementally introduce more structured documentation and refined processes.

What's most crucial is maintaining a clear line of communication with your customers or clients, ensuring transparency in your dealings, and staying organised to the best of your ability. With time, as you become more familiar with the ebb and flow of your business, incorporating best practices will become more intuitive.

Remember, every business, no matter how large or small, begins with a single step. Don't get discouraged by the journey ahead; instead, focus on making consistent, informed progress. Embrace the learning curve, and know that each day offers a new opportunity to refine and improve.

Okay, let's get back to the bookkeeping, onwards with expenses!

Mileage

You can claim mileage you drive for business reasons at 45p per mile (for cars and vans – it's a different rate if you use a motorbike or bicycle). This covers both fuel and wear and tear on your vehicle, so **no** other motor costs should be claimed in addition to mileage.

Make sure you keep a record of the miles you drive - HMRC could ask to see your records at any time. In Chapter 4, there is a mileage log, and if you need additional pages, there is a PDF of the same page available to download in the groups.

If you are registered for VAT, there is a clever little trick you can use to claim back a small portion of the VAT on the fuel element of the mileage allowance – have a look at my video:

www.elyseburns-hill.com/btb23-mileageallowance

Other Travel Costs

If you have to take a train or bus to make deliveries or to visit clients, you can include the cost of the tickets in your expenses. You can also include the cost of parking if you have had to pay for it.   Make sure you keep the tickets, especially if you pay cash, as you won't have a bank transaction to back up your claim.

Working from Home

I recommend using the "simplified expenses" calculation for this, which is a flat rate per month based on how many hours you work from home. It's quick and simple and doesn't require too much time to figure it out.

There are a couple of other ways to calculate the costs associated with working from home, but one is much more involved, and the other isn't technically correct.

Let's touch on the technically incorrect one to start with: there is a lot going around on social media about the £4 per week that you can claim – this is an old trick that accountants use to include some working-from-home expenses with minimal information available.

HMRC do not request backup records for less than £4 per week, so by including the cost at £4 per week (£208 for the whole tax year), it removes the need to save the backup for that information. There was talk about removing this £4 per week a few years ago, so I wouldn't advise using it.

The other option is to use the cost method – this works out what all your costs are and apportions it for the part of the house you are using and includes that cost in your self-assessment. It can work out much better than using simplified expenses, but it takes a lot longer to collect all your records and calculate the number you need to use.

It's a 4-step process:

1. Collect all your paperwork that proves:
   - Mortgage interest (must just be the interest element, not including any capital repayments) or rent;
   - Council Tax
   - Electricity & gas costs
   - Water costs
2. Work out how much time you are spending working from home
3. Work out how many rooms you have in your house and how many you use for business.
4. Go to the link below and put these figures into the Google Sheets calculator to find out how much you can claim as an expense in your tax calculations. (Make sure you "save a copy" of the spreadsheet, you will not be able to successfully use it if you don't).

www.elyseburns-hill.com/btb23-working-from-home

Other Sales Materials

In the realm of business, especially for those that rely heavily on direct customer interaction, visibility and brand recognition play important roles. Such visibility is often enhanced through various sales materials which not only promote the brand but also serve functional purposes.

Materials such as stickers can be used to seal packaging with a touch of personalisation, reinforcing your brand image with every product that reaches your customer. Business cards, a staple for any entrepreneur, serve as an extension of your brand, facilitating network expansion and potential client outreach. They are an essential tool for both introductions and for ensuring that potential clients or partners have your contact details.

Leaflets and brochures offer a comprehensive look into your business, services, or products. They are versatile promotional tools that can be distributed at events, storefronts, or even door-to-door. Such materials can inform potential clients about promotions, new launches, or general information about what you offer.

Car decals turn your vehicle into a mobile advertisement. Whether you're parked in a busy area or driving through town, a car decal can catch the eye of potential customers and spread awareness of your brand.

When sourcing these materials from third-party suppliers, such as Vista Print or other specialised vendors, their costs are considered business expenses. This means that when it comes time for financial reporting or tax calculations, these costs can be deducted, reducing your taxable income. It's essential to keep a detailed record of these purchases, including receipts and specifications of the order, to ensure accurate financial reporting and to take full advantage of these allowable deductions.

Telephone Costs

If you have a mobile phone specifically for your business, you can include the costs in your expenses.
If you use your personal or home phone, any *direct* costs that you've incurred you can include here i.e anything that is separately identified and charged on your phone bill – you cannot just claim the entirety of your personal phone contract.

Technically claiming a percentage of your personal contracts is not correct (although some accountants do recommend this, so clearly, it isn't enforced particularly strongly by HMRC – so it's up to you how you include this!).

If you can prove that you have upgraded to a more expensive contract so you can run your business, you could claim the difference. As long as you can show that what you're claiming is reasonable, with some form of backup if you were ever asked, you shouldn't have a problem. Even if HMRC didn't agree with you, if they can see you've put effort into trying to do it right, you likely won't get a penalty, just possibly to make up the extra tax you would have paid had you claimed less as an expense.

Broadband/Internet Costs

You'll need to find a reasonable method of dividing your costs, e.g. by the number of rooms you use for business or the amount of time you spend working from home. (They won't accept that you are working 100% of the time, so be reasonable!).

For example, if you are working 3 hours per day only while the children are at school, with 20 working days per month (on average) you are looking at 60 working hours per month.

As a percentage of total hours per month (30 times 24 = 720), you'll find 60/720 = 0.08 = 8%. If your broadband fee is £25 per month, you'll be able to claim £2 per month. Again, be reasonable and you shouldn't have a problem

Printer Costs

If you've printed anything with your home printer, you can include any ink or paper costs. Don't include the full costs of those things if you use the printer for anything not related to your business – e.g. the children's homework!

Clothing

For sole traders, the rule on clothing is that if it's branded or safety gear, you can claim it; anything else is deemed personal.

So if you buy branded t-shirts from one of your suppliers or have a hoody printed with your own name or logo on it, that is all deemed business use, and you can claim it as an expense on your tax return. prove it, don't claim it!

If you normally work on a building site or in a place where specific safety gear is needed – high-visibility clothing, lead-lined work boots etc, that is also allowable as an expense for tax.

Rain jackets, plain work shirts/blouses or walking shoes, although you might feel you need them to be able to do your job, there's no easy way of proving that they are not for personal use. If you can't prove it, don't use it.

Bank/Merchant Costs

If you have a bank account that you use purely for your business, you can claim any costs associated with running the account. Also, any merchant fees you incur processing payments from customers through processors such as PayPal, Stripe, Sum Up, Square etc. Have a watch of my video if you'd like to know more:

www.elyseburns-hill.com/btb23-payment-processors

Marketing/Advertising

If you have spent any money advertising (e.g. Facebook boost) or building/hosting a website, then you can include them as valid business expenses. Also include any costs of a stand or exhibition fee if you have a stand selling your products.

Accountancy/Professional Costs

If you pay an accountant to do your return for you, or if you pay for any bookkeeping software etc, then you can include all those costs. Oh, and the cost of this book is also a valid business expense, so keep the receipt!

Equipment To Help You Run Your Business

If you've ever acquired assets or equipment for your business, you've taken an exciting step forward. Maybe it's a shiny new computer, a trusty vehicle, or that ultra-sleek espresso machine for your cafe (because, let's be honest, caffeine fuels ambition). But with great assets comes... you guessed it, the responsibility of maintaining proper records. Let's dive into the nitty-gritty of it.

Understanding Capital Assets & Equipment:
These are significant purchases you make for your business that you expect to use over a more extended period, often more than a year. Unlike day-to-day expenses (like stationery or your daily latte), these items have a lasting value.

The Records You Should Keep:
1. Purchase Receipts: Just like you'd treasure a concert ticket of your favourite band, keep the purchase receipt safe. It should detail the cost, date of purchase, and a description of the asset.

2. Warranty Documents: If your asset comes with a warranty (and hopefully, it does!), keep this document safe. It often has vital information, including the expected life of the asset.

3. Maintenance Records: If you've given your asset some TLC, maybe in the form of repairs or maintenance, note it down. This will help you monitor its condition and could be crucial if you ever decide to sell or trade it in.

4. Depreciation Calculations: As time sails by, assets (except land) tend to decrease in value. This decrease is called 'depreciation.' Your accountant can help you calculate this, but it's essential to have records of the method you used and the annual amounts.

5. Sale or Disposal Details: If there comes a day when you part ways with your asset, record the details. Whether you've sold it, traded it in, or it's reached the end of its life, note down the date and any amounts you received or paid.

6. Logbook: Specifically for vehicles, maintain a logbook if you use it for both personal and business purposes. This logbook will help separate the business use proportion for tax deductions.

Top Tips:
- Stay Organised: Consider keeping a dedicated folder or digital file for each significant asset. With technology today, you can even snap photos of receipts and documents, storing them in cloud storage.

- Review Annually: Make it a ritual! Once a year, go through your asset records, update any changes, and ensure everything's shipshape.

Remember, your capital assets and equipment are valuable players in your business journey. By maintaining clear and comprehensive records, you're not only complying with tax regulations but also giving yourself a clear picture of your business's worth and health.

www.elyseburns-hill.com/btb23-capital-assets

What do YOU think?

I'm now going to give you a few stories of sole traders (they are made-up – any resemblance to real-life people is entirely coincidental!) and how they treated some of their expenses, I would like you to jot down some notes about whether you think their claim is a reasonable business expense. Answers are at the back of the book.

Case Study: Creative Designs by Mia

Mia, a talented graphic designer, recently left her full-time job to pursue her passion for creating bespoke wedding invitations and event stationery. Working from her home studio, Mia invested in high-quality paper stock, a professional printer, and design software. To gain inspiration and network with potential clients, Mia also attended several wedding fairs, incurring travel and booth setup costs. After a successful year, Mia decided to treat herself to a holiday, rationalising that it was a reward for her hard work and a chance to find new design inspiration. In her tax return, she claimed the holiday as a business expense, considering it partly a research trip for new ideas and trends in the wedding industry.

Did Mia correctly classify her holiday as a business expense? Consider the rules for allowable business expenses and discuss whether Mia's rationale fits within these guidelines.

_____
_____
_____
_____
_____
_____
_____
_____

Case Study: Liam's Landscaping Services

Liam is a sole trader who runs a successful landscaping business. He's a devoted father of a two-year-old and often finds himself juggling between client projects and childcare. To manage his time more efficiently, he enrolled his daughter in a local day care during his working hours. Considering that having his daughter in day care allows him uninterrupted time to focus on his business, Liam thought it might be reasonable to claim the childcare costs as a business expense. In his annual tax return, he included the day care fees under business expenses, believing they were essential for him to operate his business effectively.

Was it correct for Liam to claim his daughter's day care fees as a business expense? Reflect on the criteria for allowable business expenses in relation to personal costs.

_____
_____
_____
_____
_____
_____
_____

Case Study: Elena's Freelance Writing Venture

Elena recently started a freelance writing business, specialising in creating content for wellness and lifestyle blogs. Working from her apartment, she designated a small corner as her office space. To create a more productive environment, she purchased a new desk, an ergonomic chair, and a high-quality laptop. Elena also subscribed to various online magazines and literary journals, considering them essential for staying updated with industry trends and finding inspiration for her articles.

While completing her tax return, Elena included the cost of her home office furniture and laptop as immediate business expenses. She also claimed the subscriptions to the magazines and journals in full, reasoning that they were crucial for her business's research and development.

Did Elena correctly categorise her home office furniture, laptop, and subscription costs as immediate business expenses? Consider the rules for capital expenditures and operational expenses in your answer.

_____
_____
_____
_____
_____
_____
_____

Chapter 4: **Keeping Track - Bookkeeping**

This part of the book is like a diary for your money. It's a place where you can write down everything you earn and spend in your business, using just a pen and paper. It's perfect for anyone who likes to keep things simple and doesn't want to use a computer for this.

There is a Google Sheets version of these pages, so if you would prefer to use the tech, please find the link below. Please make sure you remember to "Save a Copy" – I can't give you access to the master copy, otherwise everyone will keep writing over each other's numbers!

www.elyseburns-hill.com/btb23-bookkeeping-google-sheet

Learning Styles

Before we get started on talking through the following pages, I want to acknowledge those of you who find this particularly stressful or whose learning styles are more geared towards watching or listening. I've recorded a video talk through these pages – it covers the same info that I've written below.

www.elyseburns-hill.com/btb23-bookkeeping-pages

Income/Expenses Statement

We start with the most important page, but you'll fill it in last. It's like the last piece of a puzzle. This page is where you'll add up all your monthly numbers at the end of the year. It'll help you see how much money you made and spent in total. The totals from this page are what goes into your tax return. If your total income is under £85,000, you can just use the total expenses figure on this summary sheet, you don't need to give HMRC the breakdown of the individual expenses.

If your income is over £85,000 then I'm afraid your job is a little more tricky as you have to breakdown the expenses into the different categories to enter on your tax return. I have made it as easy as possible for you by grouping the expenses together on the monthly bookkeeping pages in the same order as on the tax return. However, if your income is over £85,000 the chances are you'll be required to register for VAT, which requires the use of software to submit the VAT returns, so if you're reading this and you're now totally confused and worried, please reach out and we'll get you on the right track.

If you work from home, there's an extra section for you at the bottom of this first page. Remember what we talked about in Chapter 3 about the simplified expenses for working from home? You can use that info here to figure out how much you can count for working in your home.

Your Monthly Money Page

Next, you have 12 pages, one for each month of the year. Think of them as 12 chapters of your money story. Each month has spaces for every week, so you can write down what you earn each week and what you spend. You'll notice there are a couple of boxes at the bottom of each page that say "Other allowable expenses" in barely visible writing – this is so that you can add any extra lines you want; just write in what they are.

Don't worry about allocating an expense incorrectly, as long as it's included, it doesn't really matter where. We separate it out so you can start to see patterns in your spending (if you want to look) and so that we don't end up with lots of numbers in one box.

At the end of the month, you'll add these numbers across the yellow boxes and complete the blue total boxes in the income, and the orange total boxes for the expenses. When you've done that, add all the orange boxes up and put your total in the blue box at the bottom. Those three blue boxes are the figures you transfer across to the first page for each relevant month.

The Sales Log: Keeping Track of What You Sell

After the monthly pages, there's a sales log. This is where you write down everything you sell and any money you give back to customers as refunds. At the end of each week or month, you'll take the total amount you made and put it on the monthly money page. Remember to use the right date column – if you are on cash basis, you'll need to add them up based on the "Date Paid" box; if you're using traditional (accruals) accounting you'll need to add your sales up based on the invoice date. If you have no idea what I'm talking about, you're on cash basis! Have quick read of the answer to "What's the difference between 'cash basis' and 'traditional accounting'?" in chapter 2.

The Mileage Log: Counting Your Business Trips

Last, there's a page for writing down how much you travel for your business. If you use your car for work stuff, you can write down how far you go. If you need a reminder of the rules for claiming mileage, have a quick read back in chapter 3.

Let's Get Started!

So, grab your favourite pen, turn to the first monthly page, and start your journey. This is all about making things easy for you, so you know where your money is going. It's your story, and you're the one writing   it!

Self Assessment Workings 22/23
Income/Expenses Statement

Month Totals	Sales	Other Income	Expenses	WFH All.	Net Profit
April 2022					
May 2022					
June 2022					
July 2022					
August 2022					
September 2022					
October 2022					
November 2022					
December 2022					
Janaury 2023					
February 2023					
March 2023					
TOTAL					

Working from Home Allowance

Hours		0-24	25-50	51-100	101+
Flat Rate to claim		0.00	10.00	18.00	26.00

	No of hours	Flat rate
Example	34.00	10.00
April		
May		
June		
July		
August		
September		
October		
November		
December		
January		
February		
March		
TOTAL		

Self Assessment Workings 22/23
April 2022

Income/Expenses Statement	06/04/22 to 12/04/22	13/04/22 to 19/04/22	20/04/22 to 26/04/22	27/04/22 to 03/05/22		Total
Turnover/Sales						
Total Sales						
Total Other Income						
Expenses						
Cost of goods for resale						
Vehicle expenses						
Mileage/fuel						
Other travel expenses						
Wages/salaries						
Other staff costs						
Rent						
Rates						
Heat & light						
Insurance						
Repairs & maintenance - property						
Repairs & maintenance - equipment						
Accountancy costs						
Legal costs						
Other professional costs						
Interest paid						
Bank charges						
Payment processing charges						
Phone costs						
Printing & stationery costs						
Other office costs						

Self Assessment Workings 22/23
May 2022

Income/Expenses Statement	04/05/22 to 10/05/22	11/05/22 to 17/05/22	18/05/22 to 24/05/22	25/05/22 to 31/05/22		Total
Turnover/Sales						
Total Sales						
Total Other Income						
Expenses						
Cost of goods for resale						
Vehicle expenses						
Mileage/fuel						
Other travel expenses						
Wages/salaries						
Other staff costs						
Rent						
Rates						
Heat & light						
Insurance						
Repairs & maintenance - property						
Repairs & maintenance - equipment						
Accountancy costs						
Legal costs						
Other professional costs						
Interest paid						
Bank charges						
Payment processing charges						
Phone costs						
Printing & stationery costs						
Other office costs						

Self Assessment Workings 22/23
June 2022

Income/Expenses Statement	01/06/22 to 07/06/22	08/06/22 to 14/06/22	15/06/22 to 21/06/22	22/06/22 to 28/06/22		Total
Turnover/Sales						
Total Sales						
Total Other Income						
Expenses						
Cost of goods for resale						
Vehicle expenses						
Mileage/fuel						
Other travel expenses						
Wages/salaries						
Other staff costs						
Rent						
Rates						
Heat & light						
Insurance						
Repairs & maintenance - property						
Repairs & maintenance - equipment						
Accountancy costs						
Legal costs						
Other professional costs						
Interest paid						
Bank charges						
Payment processing charges						
Phone costs						
Printing & stationery costs						
Other office costs						

Self Assessment Workings 22/23
July 2022

Income/Expenses Statement	31/08/22 to 06/09/22	07/09/22 to 13/09/22	14/09/22 to 20/09/22	21/09/22 to 27/09/22	28/09/22 to 04/10/22	Total
Turnover/Sales						
Total Sales						
Total Other Income						
Expenses						
Cost of goods for resale						
Vehicle expenses						
Mileage/fuel						
Other travel expenses						
Wages/salaries						
Other staff costs						
Rent						
Rates						
Heat & light						
Insurance						
Repairs & maintenance - property						
Repairs & maintenance - equipment						
Accountancy costs						
Legal costs						
Other professional costs						
Interest paid						
Bank charges						
Payment processing charges						
Phone costs						
Printing & stationery costs						
Other office costs						

Self Assessment Workings 22/23
August 2022

Income/Expenses Statement	03/08/22 to 09/08/22	10/08/22 to 16/08/22	17/08/22 to 23/08/22	24/08/22 to 30/08/22		Total
Turnover/Sales						
Total Sales						
Total Other Income						
Expenses						
Cost of goods for resale						
Vehicle expenses						
Mileage/fuel						
Other travel expenses						
Wages/salaries						
Other staff costs						
Rent						
Rates						
Heat & light						
Insurance						
Repairs & maintenance - property						
Repairs & maintenance - equipment						
Accountancy costs						
Legal costs						
Other professional costs						
Interest paid						
Bank charges						
Payment processing charges						
Phone costs						
Printing & stationery costs						
Other office costs						

Self Assessment Workings 22/23
September 2022

Income/Expenses Statement	31/08/22 to 06/09/22	07/09/22 to 13/09/22	14/09/22 to 20/09/22	21/09/22 to 27/09/22	28/09/22 to 04/10/22	Total
Turnover/Sales						
Total Sales						
Total Other Income						
Expenses						
Cost of goods for resale						
Vehicle expenses						
Mileage/fuel						
Other travel expenses						
Wages/salaries						
Other staff costs						
Rent						
Rates						
Heat & light						
Insurance						
Repairs & maintenance - property						
Repairs & maintenance - equipment						
Accountancy costs						
Legal costs						
Other professional costs						
Interest paid						
Bank charges						
Payment processing charges						
Phone costs						
Printing & stationery costs						
Other office costs						

Self Assessment Workings 22/23
October 2022

Income/Expenses Statement	05/10/22 to 11/10/22	12/10/22 to 18/10/22	19/10/22 to 25/10/22	26/10/22 to 01/11/22		Total
Turnover/Sales						
Total Sales						
Total Other Income						
Expenses						
Cost of goods for resale						
Vehicle expenses						
Mileage/fuel						
Other travel expenses						
Wages/salaries						
Other staff costs						
Rent						
Rates						
Heat & light						
Insurance						
Repairs & maintenance - property						
Repairs & maintenance - equipment						
Accountancy costs						
Legal costs						
Other professional costs						
Interest paid						
Bank charges						
Payment processing charges						
Phone costs						
Printing & stationery costs						
Other office costs						

Self Assessment Workings 22/23
November 2022

Income/Expenses Statement	02/11/22 to 08/11/22	09/11/22 to 15/11/22	16/11/22 to 22/11/22	23/11/22 to 29/11/22	Total
Turnover/Sales					
Total Sales					
Total Other Income					
Expenses					
Cost of goods for resale					
Vehicle expenses					
Mileage/fuel					
Other travel expenses					
Wages/salaries					
Other staff costs					
Rent					
Rates					
Heat & light					
Insurance					
Repairs & maintenance - property					
Repairs & maintenance - equipment					
Accountancy costs					
Legal costs					
Other professional costs					
Interest paid					
Bank charges					
Payment processing charges					
Phone costs					
Printing & stationery costs					
Other office costs					

Self Assessment Workings 22/23
December 2022

Income/Expenses Statement	30/11/22 to 06/12/22	07/12/22 to 13/12/22	14/12/22 to 20/12/22	21/12/22 to 27/12/22	28/12/22 to 03/01/23	Total
Turnover/Sales						
Total Sales						
Total Other Income						
Expenses						
Cost of goods for resale						
Vehicle expenses						
Mileage/fuel						
Other travel expenses						
Wages/salaries						
Other staff costs						
Rent						
Rates						
Heat & light						
Insurance						
Repairs & maintenance - property						
Repairs & maintenance - equipment						
Accountancy costs						
Legal costs						
Other professional costs						
Interest paid						
Bank charges						
Payment processing charges						
Phone costs						
Printing & stationery costs						
Other office costs						

Self Assessment Workings 22/23
January 2023

Income/Expenses Statement	04/01/23 to 10/01/23	11/01/23 to 17/01/23	18/01/23 to 24/01/23	25/01/23 to 31/01/23		Total
Turnover/Sales						
Total Sales						
Total Other Income						
Expenses						
Cost of goods for resale						
Vehicle expenses						
Mileage/fuel						
Other travel expenses						
Wages/salaries						
Other staff costs						
Rent						
Rates						
Heat & light						
Insurance						
Repairs & maintenance - property						
Repairs & maintenance - equipment						
Accountancy costs						
Legal costs						
Other professional costs						
Interest paid						
Bank charges						
Payment processing charges						
Phone costs						
Printing & stationery costs						
Other office costs						

Self Assessment Workings 22/23
February 2023

Income/Expenses Statement	01/02/23 to 07/02/23	08/02/23 to 14/02/23	15/02/23 to 21/02/23	22/02/23 to 28/02/23		Total
Turnover/Sales						
Total Sales						
Total Other Income						
Expenses						
Cost of goods for resale						
Vehicle expenses						
Mileage/fuel						
Other travel expenses						
Wages/salaries						
Other staff costs						
Rent						
Rates						
Heat & light						
Insurance						
Repairs & maintenance - property						
Repairs & maintenance - equipment						
Accountancy costs						
Legal costs						
Other professional costs						
Interest paid						
Bank charges						
Payment processing charges						
Phone costs						
Printing & stationery costs						
Other office costs						

Self Assessment Workings 22/23
March 2023

Income/Expenses Statement

	01/03/23 to 07/03/23	08/03/23 to 14/03/23	15/03/23 to 21/03/23	22/03/23 to 28/03/23	29/03/23 to 05/04/23	Total
Turnover/Sales						
Total Sales						
Total Other Income						
Expenses						
Cost of goods for resale						
Vehicle expenses						
Mileage/fuel						
Other travel expenses						
Wages/salaries						
Other staff costs						
Rent						
Rates						
Heat & light						
Insurance						
Repairs & maintenance - property						
Repairs & maintenance - equipment						
Accountancy costs						
Legal costs						
Other professional costs						
Interest paid						
Bank charges						
Payment processing charges						
Phone costs						
Printing & stationery costs						
Other office costs						

Self Assessment Workings 22/23
Sales Log

Date	Invoice No	Customer	Description	Value	Date Paid

Self Assessment Workings 22/23
Sales Log

Date	Invoice No	Customer	Description	Value	Date Paid

Self Assessment Workings 22/23
Sales Log

Date	Invoice No	Customer	Description	Value	Date Paid

Self Assessment Workings 22/23
Sales Log

Date	Invoice No	Customer	Description	Value	Date Paid

Self Assessment Workings 22/23
Mileage Log

Date	Destination/Route	Reason	Total Miles

Self Assessment Workings 22/23
Mileage Log

Date	Destination/Route	Reason	Total Miles

Self Assessment Workings 22/23
Mileage Log

Date	Destination/Route	Reason	Total Miles

Self Assessment Workings 22/23
Mileage Log

Date	Destination/Route	Reason	Total Miles

Chapter 5: Introduction to Tax

Navigating the intricate web of taxation can often seem like a daunting task, especially when transitioning from traditional employment to self-employment. This chapter seeks to illuminate the complexities of the tax system, tailored specifically for those embarking on or entrenched in a self-employed journey. From understanding the fundamental differences between employment and self-employment to delving into specific allowances and reliefs, we aim to provide a comprehensive guide to empower you with the knowledge needed to manage your taxes confidently.

As we explore topics like the £1000 trading allowance, property allowance, rent-a-room relief, and the various tax bands and personal allowances, remember that taxation is more than just numbers. It's about understanding the opportunities and obligations that come with being your own boss. Each section has been crafted with clarity in mind, ensuring you grasp the essentials and are equipped to make informed decisions.

Employed Vs. Self-Employed

Navigating the intricate world of taxation can be simpler when we first understand the foundational difference between being employed and being self-employed. Both come with their own sets of responsibilities, especially when it comes to managing taxes and contributions. Let's delve deeper into these distinctions.

Employed Individuals: Delegated Tax Responsibilities

For those who have only ever been in traditional employment, the process of handling taxes can feel relatively seamless. When you're employed, your employer serves as an intermediary between you and the tax authorities. Each week/ month, before you even see your wages/salary in your bank account, your employer deducts your tax, national insurance, and possibly pension contributions. They then directly forward these amounts to the appropriate bodies, namely HMRC and pension providers.

The beauty of this system is its simplicity for the employee. Many never have to actively engage with the tax process, as everything is automatically handled. At the end of the financial year, the P60 form acts as a consolidated summary detailing your total earnings and the tax you've paid for that period. This form is crucial, especially if you need to review or verify your annual earnings and contributions.

Self-Employed Individuals: Taking Charge of Your Taxes

Transitioning to self-employment brings with it a shift in tax responsibility. Instead of relying on an employer to manage and remit your taxes, the onus is now on you. As a self-employed individual, it's imperative to maintain a meticulous record of all your earnings, expenses, and other financial transactions.

Come tax season, as we've already discussed; you'll need to complete a Self-Assessment Tax Return, submitting a detailed breakdown of your earnings to HMRC. This form will be the basis on which HMRC calculates the amount of tax you owe for the year. Unlike traditional employment, where taxes are deducted at source, in self-employment, you'll often need to make direct payments to HMRC based on your declared income and allowable expenses.

In essence, the key difference is autonomy. While being employed offers the comfort of automated tax processes, self-employment demands a proactive approach. By understanding these distinctions, you can better equip yourself to manage your financial obligations, ensuring that your entrepreneurial journey is both rewarding and compliant.

Personal Allowance and Tax Bands

Navigating the world of taxation can be daunting, but understanding key concepts such as the personal allowance and tax bands is essential for ensuring you're neither underpaying nor overpaying taxes. Here's a concise guide to get you started.

Personal Allowance:

The personal allowance is the amount of income each individual in the UK can earn tax-free every year. This amount can vary each tax year and may be influenced by factors such as your overall income or benefits received.

- How it works: If your income is below the personal allowance threshold, you don't owe any income tax. If your income exceeds this threshold, you'll be taxed only on the amount that exceeds it.

- Reduction: For high earners, the personal allowance reduces by £1 for every £2 earned over a specific threshold, until the personal allowance reaches zero.

Income Tax Bands:

Income exceeding the personal allowance is taxed according to different bands. Each band represents a portion of your income and is taxed at a specific rate. The UK's income tax bands are progressive, meaning the percentage taken increases as income does.

The bands for the 22/23 tax year are:

1. Basic Rate: This band covers income over the personal allowance up to a specified threshold. Income in this band is taxed at the basic rate, which is 20%.

2. Higher Rate: The next chunk of income, after the basic rate threshold up to a higher threshold, is taxed at the higher rate, which is 40%.

3. Additional Rate: Income over the higher threshold is taxed at the additional rate, which is 45%.

Each tax year, the specific income thresholds for each band can change, so it's crucial to stay updated with HMRC's announcements or check their official website.

Things to Remember:

- Savings and Dividends: These have different tax rates and allowances.

- Scotland: Scottish taxpayers have different tax bands and rates. If you're resident in Scotland, it's essential to be aware of these distinctions.

- National Insurance: This is separate from income tax and has its own thresholds and rates.

Understanding the personal allowance and tax bands is pivotal for every taxpayer. It ensures you know the portion of your income that remains tax-free and how the rest of your income is taxed. This knowledge is particularly useful for budgeting, financial planning, and ensuring compliance. Always keep an eye out for changes in these numbers each tax year, as they often get adjusted in line with inflation or governmental policy shifts. If you're unsure about how these apply to your situation, seeking advice from a professional or using HMRC's online tools can be beneficial.

MTD ITSA

That's a heck of an acronym, isn't it?!

It stands for **Making Tax Digital Income Tax Self-Assessment**. Before we break it down to understand it, I'm first going to tell you about HMRC's Supercomputer!

Connect, the name given to this new powerful computer system, can pull information from a number of different sources, including our government's own systems, Airbnb, eBay, Visa & Mastercard to name a few – it has even been suggested that Connect will pull information from systems that are unprotected by privacy settings – so anything that you publish publicly on Facebook could potentially be looked at by Connect. It analyses this data and creates a profile of the income of every taxpayer. When the information provided by a taxpayer differs from the information collated by Connect, it will raise a flag, which can result in an investigation into the records of the taxpayer.

It is worth mentioning at this point that there is always a possibility that your file will be pulled for an investigation, even if you have not done anything wrong. The investigation will still take time to respond to, so it really is worth spending time when you have to do your tax return each year to collect all your records together into a single bundle so that if you are ever required to send in additional information, you are able to comply quite quickly and easily.

So, now that we've talked about that, it gives a little more context to the Making Tax Digital initiative. Making Tax Digital about HMRC modernises the tax system and enables them to get more of the data behind the total numbers that are being sent in. Under MTD, tax returns will need to be submitted through MTD-compliant software so that HMRC's Connect computer can drill down into the numbers to look for patterns.

MTD for VAT is already underway and the VAT submission procedures have almost completely switched over to the MTD systems – although it took us several years longer to get there than HMRC originally anticipated. HMRC have learned a lot going through that process, so the next stage will happen more quickly.

The next group of tax returns to go into MTD is the ITSA – Income Tax for Self-Assessment – that means you! So let us look through a few things that will impact the way you will have to do things:

This process will start for taxpayers in April 2024, which seems like a long way off, but is only a tax year away!

The £1,000 Trading Allowance: A Closer Look

In Chapter 2, we briefly touched upon the concept of the £1,000 trading allowance. It's a significant provision by HMRC that can be advantageous to many, especially those just beginning their journey in self-employment or small-scale trading. Let's delve deeper into its nuances.

What is the £1,000 Trading Allowance?

Introduced by HMRC, the £1,000 trading allowance is essentially a tax-free allowance for individuals with a modest amount of business or miscellaneous income. It means that if your annual gross income from these sources is £1,000 or less, you do not need to inform HMRC, and no tax is due on it. It's designed to simplify tax for small-scale traders or those who only occasionally delve into trading activities.

How Does It Work?

1. Full Relief: If your total trading or miscellaneous income is £1,000 or less, you're automatically entitled to full relief. This means you don't need to declare this income on a tax return, making the process simpler. (Although, as we mentioned in Chapter 2, you might still want to submit a return for another reason).

2. Partial Relief: If your income exceeds £1,000, you have two choices. You can either:
   a. Deduct the £1,000 allowance from your gross income and pay tax on the excess. This method does not require you to itemize and deduct your actual expenses.
   b. Ignore the allowance and instead deduct your actual business expenses from your gross income as usual.

It's essential to calculate which method is more beneficial for you, as the best choice varies based on individual circumstances and the actual expenses incurred.

Who Can Benefit?

The trading allowance is especially beneficial for:
- Hobbyists who occasionally sell items but don't consider it a full-time business.
- Individuals who do small freelance tasks infrequently.
- People renting out a room or property occasionally, e.g., through Airbnb (though there's also a separate property allowance for this).

Key Points to Remember:

- If you use the trading allowance, you cannot deduct *any* business expenses. The £1,000 is your sole deduction.
- It's a universal figure, meaning it doesn't change regardless of the number of trades or businesses you have.

The Property Allowance: Understanding the Basics

Similar to the trading allowance we discussed previously, HMRC introduced the property allowance as a measure to simplify tax for individuals with small amounts of income from land or property. Here's what you need to know about this allowance:

What is the Property Allowance?

The property allowance is a tax exemption of up to £1,000 a year for individuals with income from property. If you have property income of more than £1,000, you can only deduct allowable property expenses or the property allowance, but not both.

How Does It Work?

1. Full Relief: If your total property income is £1,000 or less annually, you automatically qualify for full relief. This means you won't need to declare this income on your tax return, providing a hassle-free experience.

2. Partial Relief: If your property income exceeds £1,000, you can:
  a. Deduct the £1,000 property allowance from your gross property income and only pay tax on the remainder. This approach is beneficial if your actual expenses are less than £1,000.
  b. Ignore the allowance and instead calculate your taxable profit by deducting your actual property expenses from the income.

Again, the decision between these two approaches should be based on which offers a lower taxable amount, considering your specific circumstances and total expenses.

Who Can Benefit from the Property Allowance?

This allowance is particularly advantageous for:
* Individuals renting out a room in their home occasionally.
* Those who earn a nominal amount from letting a parking space, garden, or other property-related avenues.
* People with a small holiday let business.

Points to Keep in Mind:

* The property allowance cannot be used if you're benefiting from Rent a Room Relief on the same income.
* Like the trading allowance, if you use the property allowance, you cannot claim any property expenses. The £1,000 becomes your sole deduction.
* It applies to property income globally, not just within the UK. However, foreign income might have other tax implications.

The property allowance, alongside the trading allowance, exemplifies HMRC's intent to make tax matters more straightforward for individuals with minimal business or property income. But, as always, it's essential to assess your individual situation to determine the best tax strategy for you. Proper planning can ensure you're making the most of the allowances available, saving money and time in the process.

Rent a Room Relief: Maximising Your Income from Letting

Renting out a room in your home can be an excellent way to supplement your income. Fortunately, the UK government recognises the benefits of this arrangement and offers a tax incentive known as Rent a Room Relief to encourage homeowners and tenants alike. Let's delve into the details of this relief:

What is Rent a Room Relief?

Rent a Room Relief is designed for individuals who let out furnished accommodation in their only or main residence. This scheme allows you to earn up to £7,500 per year tax-free from letting out rooms in your home. If you're letting jointly, for instance, with a partner, you each can claim a tax-free allowance of up to £3,750.

How Does It Work?

1. Automatic Exemption: If your gross receipts (i.e., before expenses) from letting don't exceed the threshold, the income is automatically exempt from tax, and you don't need to do anything.

2. Above the Threshold: If your gross receipts are more than the limit, you have two options:
   a. Pay tax on the actual profit from letting (gross receipts minus allowable expenses)
   b. Pay tax on the gross receipts above the allowance – without deducting expenses.

You'll need to inform HMRC which method you want to use (this can be done on the tax return). If you don't, the automatic method will be the actual profit from letting.

Who Can Benefit from Rent a Room Relief?

- Homeowners renting out a spare room or a floor in their main residence.
- Tenants, subject to landlord approval, subletting a room in the property they rent.
- Those running a bed and breakfast or guest house, as long as it's your main residence.

Points to Keep in Mind:

- The scheme does not apply to homes converted into separate flats.
- You cannot claim Rent a Room Relief if the accommodation is not part of your main home at the time of renting or if the home was not used by the tenant as their main or only residence.
- The relief cannot be combined with the property allowance. If you claim Rent a Room Relief, you cannot also deduct £1,000 from property income using the property allowance.
- If you opt into the scheme, you can't deduct any expenses related to the letting (e.g., utility bills, insurance, repairs).

Rent a Room Relief offers a fantastic opportunity for homeowners and tenants to capitalise on unused space in their main residence. If you're considering letting a room in your home or already doing so, understanding this relief ensures you make the most of your income, without unnecessary tax implications. As with any tax-related decision, it's always wise to assess your individual situation carefully and seek professional advice if unsure.

Seek Professional Advice

This chapter is just an introduction to tax; there is a lot not covered here. There is a lot of information available on the HMRC website, but please don't be afraid to book an appointment with an accountant to make sure you are doing the right thing. Sometimes the peace of mind that comes with *knowing* you're doing the right thing rather than *guessing* at it, is worth the cost of an hour meeting.

Chapter 6: Submitting Your Tax Return

Submitting your tax return isn't as scary as you think. Just follow the instructions and do the best you can. If you have done everything in good faith and to the best of your ability, you are unlikely to be penalised if you have done anything wrong. The problem comes when you are seen to be deliberately manipulating your numbers so that you pay less tax.

There are two ways to file your tax return – paper form or online filing. If you want to file your tax return on paper (I know some people just prefer good old-fashioned pen and paper!), you'll need to make sure you've completed it and submitted it by 31 October 2023. If you file online using Government Gateway, you have until 31 January 2024.

In this chapter, I provide screenshots of online filing simply because more and more people are filing online these days. All the same information is asked on the paper form; it just looks slightly different. If you turn to the end of the chapter, I have included a copy of the paper form with a few supplementary pages as part of the quiz.   By working through this chapter in its entirety, you will have all the information you need to successfully complete your tax return whether its online or on paper.

Logging In

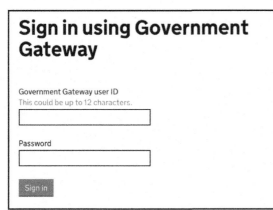

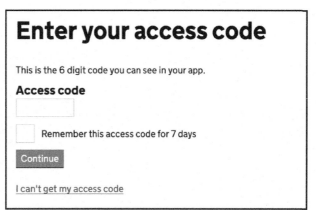

When you've logged in to your account, you'll see something like the screen below. You'll need to click on the Self-Assessment link on the right-hand side.

You can use this service if in the tax year ending 5 April 2019 you received:

- employment income
- self-employment income
- partnership income
- UK property income ?
- pensions
- UK interest, dividends etc ?
- foreign income ?
- Capital Gains ?
- **Child Benefit** for earners over £50,000 ?

It is very important that you enter the correct amount in the appropriate box on the return. Errors or mistakes can lead to you being asked to pay the wrong amount of tax, and can take time to correct.

Find out more about using the File a return service

This page is also available in Welsh (Cymraeg).

Start Now >

You will be then asked to check that you should be using this service – and as you have self-employment income, you will, so click on start.

You might also need passport or P6o to be able to log on – if you haven't setup an access code (using either your mobile phone number or the HMRC app) then it asks for other forms of ID when logging in. If you have any problems logging on, your best bet is to give the tax office a ring.

Contacting HMRC
The phone number for the Self-Assessment office is 0300 200 3310 and the textphone is 0300 200 3319. The lines are open Monday to Friday, 8 am to 6 pm, and are closed on weekends and bank holidays.

Here are a couple of tips that will be useful when calling HMRC:
- Call as soon after 8 am as you are able, the lines are relatively free between 8 & 9 am and they get busier as the day gets on.
- Have your details to hand, particularly your National Insurance number – you will be asked security questions to ensure they have the authority to talk to you

Tailoring Your Return

Once you're logged in and can access your return, it will ask for some information about you. I won't go through the answers for this because, hopefully, you'll know the answers to these questions!

The next stage is to start tailoring your return. You can come back and change this at any time before you submit your return.

Most of the questions are Yes or No questions, it's just so that the system doesn't overwhelm you by trying to give you all the questions. It will ask you about what types of income you have and just show you those sections to complete. If you're not sure about something, click yes and then go checkout that section – you'll realise pretty quickly if it's not relevant to you, so you can come back and change your answer to no so that it hides the section again. Equally, if you realise your return hasn't asked you about something, then you'll need to come back and review your answers to the tailoring questions.

Page 1

Employment Income
The form asks whether you were an employee during the tax year and, if so, what the details and earnings from that employment were. All the information you need for this section will be on the P6o issued to you by your employer. For more information on employment income, please see Chapter 5.

Self-Employment Income
If you worked for yourself or were a subcontractor working in the construction industry, and your turnover was more than £1000 across all your self-employed businesses, you'll need to complete the Self-Employment section. Please see Chapter 5 for more on the £1000 Trading Allowance.

You will need to complete separate self-employment pages for each different self-employed business you run, so if you run a part-time babysitting business and a graphic design business, you'll need to complete these numbers separately.

There are 2 different types of self-employment pages. You can use the "short" pages if your turnover was below £85,000 for the tax year and is relatively straightforward, or if it is more complex and your turnover was above £85,000, then you'll need to use the full pages.

Income from UK Property or Land

If you own or lease property or land from which you collect rent, you'll need to complete the UK property pages. This also includes furnished holiday lets (e.g. Airbnb) and also when you let out rooms within your own home (except where you provide meals or other services, where it becomes self-employment...I know, it's maze!).

There is another allowance for property income, which is very similar to the Trading Allowance, and is called (surprise!) the Property Income Allowance.

Foreign Earnings

I'm not going to spend long on foreign income, if you do have foreign income, your tax return starts to head towards the complex end. Depending on which country that income was earned in, whether they have double taxation relief, where you physically were when that money was earned, and whether you are resident her or in the other country, makes a difference on how it's accounted for. My advice would be to have a chat with an accountant with knowledge of the tax rules in the country where you earned your income.

Capital Gains

The chargeable gains section is asking about disposal of large assets (worth more than £49,200) it has increased in value (where the gain was more than £12,300), for example a house or property, maybe a family heirloom. If you might have something like this, I'd recommend getting an appointment with an Accountant as you'll want to make sure you're treating it correctly. A separate capital gains return should be filed within 60 days of selling a property if the completion date was after 27th October 2021. If you think you have any capital gains to report, I'd advise a quick chat with an accountant so you know you're doing the right thing.

Page 2

Interest income

This could be interest from your bank accounts or any other interest producing financial asset. Usually you will be provided with a statement at the end of each tax year – if you're not provided with one automatically, you should be able to request one.

Dividend income

Dividends come from owning shares in companies. This could be a small to medium-sized Limited Company, or it could be shares held in a big public company like Amazon, Tesco or Apple. Whenever you receive a dividend, you will receive a dividend voucher telling you the information you need to include in your tax return. It is unlikely companies will give you a statement at the end of the tax year, so you'll need to dig out the dividend vouchers you were sent when the dividend was issued.

UK pensions, annuities or state benefits

If you receive a state pension, occupational pension, retirement annuity, or incapacity benefit, you will need to check whether your income is taxable. Most pensions are taxable, and some state benefits are also taxable. The quickest way might be to call HMRC to check your specific situation.

Child Benefit

Child benefit is available to those with children, but when you make the claim, they don't check your income. When any adult in the household is earning more than £50,000, whether they are a parent of the child or not, they will need to make a payment back to the government. How much you have to pay back depends on exactly how much you're earning; it' calculated on a sliding scale between £50,000 and £60,000. If your income is over £60,000, you will have to pay back 100% of the child benefit you've claimed in the year. It might be that this could be advantageous to you as you can use that money during the year and then pay it back with your tax return, or you can phone the child benefit department and ask them to stop the payments. The important part to note is that even if the person earning over £50,000 is employed and doesn't otherwise need to submit a tax return, they will need to submit one to pay back the benefit charge. I've heard of far too many stories of HMRC coming to claim back over-paid child benefits from parents who had no idea they were claiming when they shouldn't have been, and they've had to find thousands to pay back.

Other UK Income

I don't often see "other income' for my clients, but it does occasionally happen, it's pretty much any income you've had that doesn't fit into another category, for example, any earnings from work that weren't taxed at the time you received them, like tips. Another example is payments from a personal insurance policy for sickness or disability benefits. There are loads of examples of income you might have received that don't fit anywhere else in the tax return. Consider any time you have received money and whether it should be taxed. If you're not sure, ask in the Facebook group.

Losses in the Year

If you have any losses from casual income or commissions in the tax year that you need to report that isn't covered elsewhere in the return, you'll need to complete this section, so click yes. If you have self-employment losses, that will be covered in the self-employment section, so click no.

Pension Savings

If you have pension savings that may be taxable, click yes here.

Page 3

Pension/Annuity Contributions

If you made contributions to a personal pension or retirement annuity (not including payments that went through your payslip to your employer's pension scheme, as this has already been dealt with correctly), you'll need to click yes and provide more information.

Charitable Giving

This is about whether you gave any money to charity (specifically thinking about whether you said yes to gift aid at any point during the year).

Married Couple's Allowance

For those of you who were born before 6th April 1935, you might be eligible to claim married couple's allowance, so click yes here.

Personal Allowance Transfer to Spouse

If you earn below the tax threshold (£12,570 for 22/23 tax year) and your spouse earns above the threshold, you can transfer 10% of your personal allowance to your spouse or civil partner so they have a larger personal allowance before tax kicks in, which at 20% can mean a £250 saving. Make sure you understand what you are doing here before you click yes – talk it through on the Facebook group if you like.

Other Tax Reliefs and Deductions

If you want to claim any other tax reliefs and deductions – you'll probably know if you've done something in the year that this applies to, so if you don't, just click no.

Previous Tax Year Refunds

If you've had any 21/22 tax refunded or offset by HMRC or the Job Centre. You will receive a notification if this is the case. This is not for refunds that came in an earlier year or from an employer.

Tax Adviser

"Did you have a tax adviser?" – I am not your adviser, and this book does not serve as advice – if anything, I consider myself to be a translator (from HMRC gobbledygook to English!). Please see the disclaimer at the front of the book! If you did use a tax adviser, then click yes; if you didn't, click no;

Tax Avoidance

This question is about whether you used a tax avoidance scheme. There is a difference between tax avoidance and tax evasion – tax evasion is illegal and can be done by not declaring income and not paying tax when you should have done. Tax avoidance is not illegal but is generally quite an aggressive interpretation of the tax law – what the big companies like Costa, Apple and Google do could be tax avoidance. It goes beyond simple tax planning, so I expect your answer will probably be no to this one.

Disguised Remuneration Schemes

Disguised remuneration avoidance schemes would relate to the issue that's been in the news recently about all these umbrella schemes that people used to pay themselves. Hopefully you'll know if this applies to you.

Me, Myself and I

The final question is about whether you are completing the return yourself – the answer is probably yes!

Fill in your Return

First page, you'll see what documentation you'll need to complete your return. Obviously, you won't necessarily need all of it, when you have finished tailoring your return, you'll be told exactly what you need.

Fill in your return
Check your progress

To complete your return you may need the following documents:

- P60 or P45 (Part 1A)
- P11D or equivalent information from your employer
- Profit or loss accounts
- Records of business receipts and business expenses
- Bank statements or any receipts from the charity
- 2018 to 2019 and 2019 to 2020 Notices of Coding

This section provides you with an overview of what pages make up your tailored return.
✔ A tick means you have entered information into this page. To change this please select from the list below.
✚ A plus means you have yet to enter information into this page.

Employment

The next section is about employment details – so this will be about any employment that you had during the tax year. If it doesn't show up, and you were employed, you'll need to go back and adjust your answers in the tailoring section. For each employed job you had, you should have either a P60 (issued to all employees at the end of each tax year) or a P45 (issued to all employees as they leave employment). The P60 and P45 both show you the total income you earned in the tax year from that employer, and the total tax you paid.

Self-Employment

Next comes your self-employment, during the tailoring section, you will have advised how many different self-employed businesses you run, so if you said 1, it will give you 1 page to complete, if you said 2, it will give you 2 pages to complete...and so on. If you completed either the pages in this book or the spreadsheet, you just pick up the relevant numbers and type them straight into the return.

There is one box asking for the total amount of taxable income, so you pop your total sales figure for the year into that box. There is another box for total "Other Income", if you have a total for that, then pop that number in.

If your total income is below £85,000, then you don't need to complete the individual boxes for the different types of expenses; you can put in a single total figure for all your expenses. If you used the pages in this book and you claimed the working from home allowance, you'll need to add the working from home allowance to the total expenses and then put that combined figure into the tax return.

If you had losses from last year and profit this year, you can use those losses from last year to offset this year's taxable profit and reduce your tax bill for this year.

National Insurance Contributions

National Insurance Class 2 is payable if you earn over a certain amount, so this section will take you through if you have to pay any or if you want to voluntarily pay any.

Over/Underpaid Taxes

The last but one page asks you for information about your tax coding and whether you've over/underpaid tax through your coding.

Final Summary
The final page is asking you to check your return and shows you all the calculations.

There is a lot of information asked for in the tax return, and everyone's earnings situation is slightly different. I've tried to cover all the most common parts here, but if there's anything I don't cover that does apply to you, please ask about it in the group – as I see questions coming up I can see whether a particular thing is being asked about a lot, and I can add a section here in the book. Equally, if I don't explain something in enough detail, again, ask, because then I can see I'll need to add more detail for a future edition of the book.

The Great Tax Return Quiz!

I know you think I can't turn a tax return into a fun game, but you'd be wrong! ...Ok, 'fun' might be a little strong, but let's just be light-hearted about this, shall we?!

Your mission, should you choose to accept it, is to answer these questions using the paper tax return that follows them. You could just write the answers in the book, *OR* you could send these answers to me and be in with a chance to win a prize.

The deadline is midnight on 31 January 2024. Please follow the link below or use the QR code to access the Google form to submit your answers, and please note the fine print for the terms of the competition is also there. Good luck!

Competition entry link: https://forms.gle/iVftborF99cKE2CT8

The Quiz Questions

Question 1: What amount is listed as the total income from self-employment?

Question 2: Find the taxable property profits before expenses. What is the value?

Question 3: Identify whether a High Income Child Benefit Charge will be applied.

Question 4: How much total interest income is reported on the tax return?

Question 5: Does the tax return indicate a Marriage Allowance transfer from the spouse?

Question 6: Are there any charitable contributions listed on the tax return?

HM Revenue & Customs

Tax Return 2023

Tax year 6 April 2022 to 5 April 2023 (2022–23)

UTR   3872375403
NINO QQ 12 34 56
Employer reference

Date

HM Revenue and Customs office address

⌐   ¬

L   ⌐

Telephone

Issue address

⌐   ¬
THE BAKERY
PUDDING LANE
LONDON
EC3R 8AB

L   ⌐

For
Reference

Your tax return

This notice requires you, by law, to make a return of your taxable income and capital gains, and any documents requested, for the year from 6 April 2022 to 5 April 2023

Deadlines

We must receive your tax return by these dates:
• if you're using a paper return – by 31 October 2023 (or 3 months after the date of this notice if that's later)
• if you're filing a return online – by 31 January 2024 (or 3 months after the date of this notice if that's later)

If your return is late you'll be charged a £100 penalty. If your return is more than 3 months late, you'll be charged daily penalties of £10 a day.

If you pay late you'll be charged interest and a late payment penalty.

Most people file online

It's quick and easy to file online. Get started by typing www.gov.uk/log-in-file-self-assessment-tax-return into your internet browser address bar to go directly to our official website.

Do not use a search website to find HMRC services online. If you have not sent a tax return online before, why not join the 92% of people who already do it online? It's easy, secure and available 24 hours a day and you can also sign up for email alerts and online messages to help you manage your tax affairs.

To file on paper, please fill in this form using the following rules:
• enter your figures in whole pounds – ignore the pence
• round down income and round up expenses and tax paid, it is to your benefit
• if a box does not apply, please leave it blank – do not strike through empty boxes or write anything else

Starting your tax return

Before you start to fill it in, look through your tax return to make sure there is a section for all your income and claims – you may need some separate supplementary pages (see page TR 2 and the Tax Return notes).

For help filling in this form, go to www.gov.uk/taxreturnforms and read the notes and helpsheets.

Your personal details

1 **Your date of birth** – it helps get your tax right
DD MM YYYY

2 7   0 6   1 9 8 8

2 **Your name and address** – if it is different from what is on the front of this form, please write the correct details underneath the wrong ones and put the date you changed address below DD MM YYYY

3 **Your phone number**

0 7 8 1 1 1 2 2 3 4 5

4 **Your National Insurance number** – leave blank if the correct number is shown above

What makes up your tax return

To make a complete return of your taxable income and gains for the year to 5 April 2023 you may need to complete some separate supplementary pages. Answer the following questions by putting 'X' in the 'Yes' or 'No' box.

1 Employment

Were you an employee, director, office holder or agency worker in the year to 5 April 2023? Please read the notes before answering. Fill in a separate 'Employment' page for each employment, directorship and so on. On each 'Employment' page you complete, enter any other payments, expenses or benefits related to that employment. Say how many 'Employment' pages you are completing in the 'Number' box below.

Yes ☐   No ☒   Number ☐

2 Self-employment

If you worked for yourself (on your 'own account' or in self-employment) in the year to 5 April 2023, read the notes to decide if you need to fill in the 'Self-employment' pages. You may not need to if this income is up to £1,000.

Do you need to fill in the 'Self-employment' pages?

Fill in a separate 'Self-employment' page for each business.

On each 'Self-employment' page you complete, enter any payments or expenses related to that business. Say how many businesses you had in the 'Number' box below. (Answer 'Yes' if you were a 'Name' at Lloyd's.)

Yes ☒   No ☐   Number **1**

3 Partnership

Were you in a partnership? Fill in a separate 'Partnership' page for each partnership you were a partner in and say how many partnerships you had in the 'Number' box below.

Yes ☐   No ☒   Number ☐

4 UK property

If you received income from UK property (including rents and other income from land you own or lease out), read the notes to decide if you need to fill in the 'UK property' pages. You may not need to if this income is up to £1,000.
Do you need to fill in the 'UK property' pages?

Yes ☒   No ☐

5 Foreign

If you:
• were entitled to any foreign income
• have, or could have, received (directly or indirectly) income, or a capital payment or benefit from a person abroad as a result of any transfer of assets
• want to claim relief for foreign tax paid
read the notes to decide if you need to fill in the 'Foreign' pages. You may not need to if your only foreign income was from land and property abroad up to £1,000.

Do you need to fill in the 'Foreign' pages?

Yes ☐   No ☒

6 Trusts etc

Did you receive, or are you treated as having received, income from a trust, settlement or the residue of a deceased person's estate? This does not include cash lump sums/transfer of assets, otherwise known as capital distributions, received under a will.

Yes ☐   No ☒

7 Capital Gains Tax summary

If you sold or disposed of any assets (for example, stocks, shares, land and property, a business), or had any chargeable gains, read the notes to decide if you have to fill in the 'Capital Gains Tax summary' page. If you do, you must also provide separate computations.

Do you need to fill in the 'Capital Gains Tax summary' page and provide computations?

Yes ☐   No ☒   Computation(s) provided ☐

8 Residence, remittance basis etc

Were you, for all or part of the year to 5 April 2023, one or more of the following:
• not resident
• not domiciled in the UK and claiming the remittance basis
• dual resident in the UK and another country?

Yes ☐   No ☒

9 Additional information

Some less common kinds of income and tax reliefs, for example, Married Couple's Allowance, Life insurance gains, chargeable event gains, Seafarer's Earnings Deduction and details of disclosed tax avoidance schemes, should be returned on the 'Additional information' pages. Do you need to fill in the 'Additional information' pages?

Yes ☐   No ☒

If you need more pages

If you answered 'Yes' to any of questions 1 to 9, please check to see if within this return, there's a page dealing with that kind of income or gain. If there's not, you'll need separate supplementary pages. Do you need to get and fill in separate supplementary pages?

Yes ☒   No ☐

If 'Yes', go to www.gov.uk/taxreturnforms to download them.

SA100 2023   Page TR 2

Income

Interest and dividends from UK banks and building societies

1 **Taxed UK interest** – the net amount after tax has been taken off - read the notes

£ _____ . 0 0

2 **Untaxed UK interest** – amounts which have not had tax taken off - read the notes

£ _____ 1 4 . 0 0

3 **Untaxed foreign interest (up to £2,000)** – amounts which have not had tax taken off - read the notes

£ _____ . 0 0

4 **Dividends from UK companies** – the amount received - read the notes

£ _____ . 0 0

5 **Other dividends** – the amount received - read the notes

£ _____ . 0 0

6 **Foreign dividends (up to £2,000)** – the amount in sterling after foreign tax was taken off. Do not include this amount in the 'Foreign' pages

£ _____ . 0 0

7 **Tax taken off foreign dividends** – the sterling equivalent

£ _____ . 0 0

UK pensions, annuities and other state benefits received

8 **State Pension** – amount you were entitled to receive in the year, **not the weekly or 4-weekly amount** - read the notes

£ _____ . 0 0

9 **State Pension lump sum** – the gross amount of any lump sum - read the notes

£ _____ . 0 0

10 **Tax taken off box 9**

£ _____ . 0 0

11 **Pensions (other than State Pension), retirement annuities and taxable lump sums treated as pensions** – the gross amount. Tax taken off goes in box 12

£ _____ . 0 0

12 **Tax taken off box 11**

£ _____ . 0 0

13 **Taxable Incapacity Benefit and contribution-based Employment and Support Allowance** - read the notes

£ _____ . 0 0

14 **Tax taken off Incapacity Benefit in box 13**

£ _____ . 0 0

15 **Jobseeker's Allowance**

£ _____ . 0 0

16 **Total of any other taxable State Pensions and benefits**

£ _____ . 0 0

Other UK income not included on supplementary pages

Do not use this section for income that should be returned on supplementary pages. Share schemes, gilts, stock dividends, life insurance gains and certain other kinds of income go on the 'Additional information' pages.

17 **Other taxable income** – before expenses and tax taken off

£ _____ . 0 0

18 **Total amount of allowable expenses** – read the notes

£ _____ . 0 0

19 **Any tax taken off box 17**

£ _____ . 0 0

20 **Benefit from pre-owned assets** - read the notes

£ _____ . 0 0

21 **Description of income in boxes 17 and 20** – if there's not enough space here please give details in the 'Any other information' box, box 19, on page TR 7

_____

Tax reliefs

Paying into registered pension schemes and overseas pension schemes

Do not include payments you make to your employer's pension scheme which are deducted from your pay before tax or payments made by your employer. If your contributions and other pension inputs are more than the Annual Allowance, you should also fill in boxes 10 to 12 on page Ai 4 of the 'Additional information' pages.

1 Payments to registered pension schemes where basic rate tax relief will be claimed by your pension provider (called 'relief at source'). Enter the payments and basic rate tax

£ · 0 0

1.1 Total of any 'one-off' payments in box 1

£ · 0 0

2 Payments to a retirement annuity contract where basic rate tax relief will not be claimed by your provider

£ · 0 0

3 Payments to your employer's scheme which were not deducted from your pay before tax – this will be unusual – read the notes

£ · 0 0

4 Payments to an overseas pension scheme, which is not UK-registered, which are eligible for tax relief and were not deducted from your pay before tax

£ · 0 0

Charitable giving

5 Gift Aid payments made in the year to 5 April 2023

£ 8 9 · 0 0

6 Total of any 'one-off' payments in box 5

£ · 0 0

7 Gift Aid payments made in the year to 5 April 2023 but treated as if made in the year to 5 April 2022

£ · 0 0

8 Gift Aid payments made after 5 April 2023 but to be treated as if made in the year to 5 April 2023

£ · 0 0

9 Value of qualifying shares or securities gifted to charity

£ · 0 0

10 Value of qualifying land and buildings gifted to charity

£ · 0 0

11 Value of qualifying investments gifted to non-UK charities in boxes 9 and 10

£ · 0 0

12 Gift Aid payments to non-UK charities in box 5

£ · 0 0

Blind Person's Allowance

13 If you're registered blind, or severely sight impaired, and your name is on a local authority or other register, put 'X' in the box

14 Enter the name of the local authority or other register

15 If you want your spouse's, or civil partner's, surplus allowance, put 'X' in the box

16 If you want your spouse, or civil partner, to have your surplus allowance, put 'X' in the box

ℹ️ Other less common reliefs are on the 'Additional information' pages.

SA100 2023   **Page TR 4**

Student Loan and Postgraduate Loan repayments

Please read the notes before filling in boxes 1 to 3.

1 If you've received notification from Student Loans Company that your repayment of an Income Contingent Loan was due before 6 April 2023, put 'X' in the box. We'll use your plan and or loan type to calculate amounts due

2 If your employer has deducted Student Loan repayments enter the amount deducted

£ __ . 0 0

3 If your employer has deducted Postgraduate Loan repayments enter the amount deducted

£ __ . 0 0

High Income Child Benefit Charge

Please read the notes before filling in this section. Only fill in this section if all of the following apply:

- your income was over £50,000
- you or your partner (if you have one) got Child Benefit (this also applies if someone else claims Child Benefit for a child who lives with you and pays you or your partner for the child's upkeep)
- couples only – your income was higher than your partner's

1 Enter the total amount of Child Benefit you and your partner got for the year to 5 April 2023

£ 2 6 1 . 0 0

2 Enter the number of children you and your partner got Child Benefit for on 5 April 2023

1

3 Enter the date that you and your partner stopped getting all Child Benefit payments if this was before 6 April 2023
DD MM YYYY

Incorrectly claimed coronavirus support scheme payments

Please read the notes before filling in this section. Only fill in this section if you incorrectly claimed any payments from the Coronavirus Job Retention Scheme or from any other applicable HMRC coronavirus support scheme and you still need to tell HMRC.

1 Amount of HMRC coronavirus support scheme payments incorrectly claimed

£ __ . 0 0

Marriage Allowance

Please read the notes. If your income for the year ended 5 April 2023 was less than £12,570 you can transfer £1,260 of your Personal Allowance to your spouse or civil partner to reduce the amount of tax they pay if all of the following apply:

- you were married to, or in a civil partnership with, the same person for all or part of the tax year
- you were both born on or after 6 April 1935
- your spouse or civil partner's income was not taxed at the higher rate

Fill in this section if you want to make the transfer.

1 Your spouse or civil partner's first name

2 Your spouse or civil partner's last name

3 Your spouse or civil partner's National Insurance number

4 Your spouse or civil partner's date of birth DD MM YYYY

5 Date of marriage or civil partnership DD MM YYYY

Finishing your tax return

ℹ Calculating your tax – if we receive this paper tax return by 31 October 2023 or if you file online, we'll do the calculation for you and tell you how much you have to pay (or what your repayment will be) before 31 January 2024. We'll add the amount due to your Self Assessment Statement, together with any other amounts due.

Do not enter payments on account, or other payments you've made towards the amounts due, on your tax return. We'll deduct these on your Self Assessment Statement. If you want to calculate your tax, ask us for the 'Tax calculation summary' pages and notes. The notes will help you work out any tax due, or repayable, and if payments on account are necessary.

Tax refunded or set off

1 **If you've had any 2022–23 Income Tax refunded or set off by us or Jobcentre Plus, enter the amount** - read the notes

£ [   ] . 0 0

If you have not paid enough tax

We recommend you pay any tax due electronically. Read the notes.

2 **If you owe less than £3,000 for the 2022–23 tax year (excluding Class 2 NICs) and you send us your paper tax return by 31 October, or 30 December 2023 if you file online, we'll try to collect the tax through your wages or pension by adjusting your 2024–25 tax code. If you do not want us to do this, put 'X' in the box** - read the notes

3 **If you owe tax on savings, casual earnings and/or the High Income Child Benefit Charge for the 2023–24 tax year, we'll try to collect it through your wages or pension by adjusting your 2023–24 tax code. If you do not want us to do this, put 'X' in the box** - read the notes

If you have paid too much tax

To claim a repayment, fill in boxes 4 to 14 below. If you paid your tax by credit or debit card, we'll always try to repay back to your card first before making any repayment as requested by you below. Please allow up to 4 weeks for any repayment to reach you before contacting us.

4 **Name of bank or building society**

5 **Name of account holder (or nominee)**

6 **Branch sort code**

7 **Account number**

8 **Building society reference number**

9 **If you do not have a bank or building society account, or if you want us to send a cheque to you or to your nominee, put 'X' in the box**

10 **If you've entered a nominee's name in box 5, put 'X' in the box**

11 **If your nominee is your tax adviser, put 'X' in the box**

12 **Nominee's address**

13 **and postcode**

14 **To authorise your nominee to receive any repayment, you must sign in the box. A photocopy of your signature will not do**

Your tax adviser, if you have one

This section is optional. Please read the notes about authorising your tax adviser.

15 Your tax adviser's name

16 Their phone number

17 The first line of their address including the postcode

Postcode

18 The reference your adviser uses for you

Any other information

19 Please give any other information in this space

Signing your form and sending it back

Please fill in this section and sign and date the declaration at box 22.

20 If this tax return contains provisional figures, put 'X' in the box

20.1 If any of your businesses received coronavirus support payments (such as CJRS) you must put 'X' in the box to declare that they have been included when calculating profits in the period of this return

21 If you're enclosing separate supplementary pages, put 'X' in the box

22 Declaration

I declare that the information I've given on this tax return and any supplementary pages is correct and complete to the best of my knowledge and belief.

I understand that I may have to pay financial penalties and face prosecution if I give false information.

Signature

Lucy Farriner

Date DD MM YYYY

| 0 | 8 | | 0 | 5 | | 2 | 0 | 2 | 3 |

23 If you've signed on behalf of someone else, enter the capacity. For example, executor, receiver

24 Enter the name of the person you've signed for

25 If you filled in boxes 23 and 24 enter your name

26 and your address

Postcode

HM Revenue & Customs

Self-employment (short)

Tax year 6 April 2022 to 5 April 2023 (2022–23)

Please read the 'Self-employment (short) notes' to check if you should use this page or the 'Self-employment (full)' page.

For help filling in this form, go to www.gov.uk/taxreturnforms and read the notes and helpsheets.

Your name
LUCY FARRINER

Your Unique Taxpayer Reference (UTR)
3 8 7 2 3 7 5 4 0 3

Business details

1 Description of business
BAKERY

2 Postcode of your business address
E C 3 R 8 A B

3 If your business name, description, address or postcode have changed in the last 12 months, put 'X' in the box and give details in the 'Any other information' box of your tax return

4 If you are a foster carer or shared lives carer, put 'X' in the box

5 If your business started after 5 April 2022, enter the start date DD MM YYYY

6 If your business ceased before 6 April 2023, enter the final date of trading DD MM YYYY

7 Date your books or accounts are made up to
0 5 0 4 2 0 2 3

8 If you used cash basis, money actually received and paid out, to calculate your income and expenses put 'X' in the box
X

Business income – if your annual business turnover was below £85,000

9 Your turnover – the takings, fees, sales or money earned by your business
£ 7 9 0 8 4 . 0 0

10 Any other business income not included in box 9 – also include any COVID support payments such as CJRS
£ 3 8 7 3 . 0 0

10.1 Trading income allowance – read the notes
£ . 0 0

Allowable business expenses

If your annual turnover was below £85,000 you may just put your total expenses in box 20, rather than filling in the whole section.

11 Costs of goods bought for resale or goods used
£ . 0 0

12 Car, van and travel expenses – after private use proportion
£ . 0 0

13 Wages, salaries and other staff costs
£ . 0 0

14 Rent, rates, power and insurance costs
£ . 0 0

15 Repairs and maintenance of property and equipment
£ . 0 0

16 Accountancy, legal and other professional fees
£ . 0 0

17 Interest and bank and credit card financial charges
£ . 0 0

18 Phone, fax, stationery and other office costs
£ . 0 0

19 Other allowable business expenses – client entertaining costs are not an allowable expense
£ . 0 0

20 Total allowable expenses – total of boxes 11 to 19
£ 3 2 3 1 4 . 0 0

Net profit or loss

21 **Net profit** – if your business income is more than your expenses (if box 9 + box 10 minus box 20 is positive)	22 **Or, net loss** – if your expenses exceed your business income (if box 20 minus (box 9 + box 10) is positive)
£ 5 0 6 4 3 · 0 0	£ · 0 0

Tax allowances for certain buildings, vehicles and equipment (capital allowances)

Do not include the cost of these in your business expenses.

23 **Annual Investment Allowance**	25.1 **The Structures and Buildings Allowance**
£ · 0 0	£ · 0 0
24 **Allowance for small balance of unrelieved expenditure**	25.2 **Freeport Structures and Buildings Allowance**
£ · 0 0	£ · 0 0
24.1 **Zero-emission car allowance**	26 **Total balancing charges** – for example, where you have disposed of items for more than their tax value
£ · 0 0	£ · 0 0
25 **Other capital allowances**	
£ · 0 0	

Calculating your taxable profits

Your taxable profit may not be the same as your net profit. Please read the 'Self-employment (short) notes' to see if you need to make any adjustments and fill in the boxes which apply to arrive at your taxable profit for the year.

27 **Goods and/or services for your own use**	29 **Loss brought forward from earlier years set off against this year's profits** – up to the amount in box 28
£ · 0 0	£ · 0 0
28 **Net business profit for tax purposes (if box 21 + box 26 + box 27 minus (boxes 22 to 25.2) is positive).** Or if you've completed box 10.1 (box 21 + box 26 + box 27 minus box 10.1)	30 **Any other business income not included in box 9 or box 10**
£ · 0 0	£ · 0 0

Total taxable profits or net business loss

If your total profits from all Self-employments and Partnerships for 2022–23 are less than £6,725, you do not have to pay Class 2 National Insurance contributions, but you may want to pay voluntarily (box 36) to protect your rights to certain benefits.

31 **Total taxable profits from this business** (if box 28 + box 30 minus box 29 is positive)	32 **Net business loss for tax purposes (if boxes 22 to 25.2 minus (box 21 + box 26 + box 27) is positive)**
£ 5 0 6 4 3 · 0 0	£ · 0 0

Losses, Class 2 and Class 4 National Insurance contributions (NICs) and CIS deductions

If you've made a loss for tax purposes (box 32), read the 'Self-employment (short) notes' and fill in boxes 33 to 35 as appropriate.

33 **Loss from this tax year set off against other income for 2022–23**	36 **If your total profits for 2022–23 are less than £6,725 and you choose to pay Class 2 NICs voluntarily, put 'X' in the box**
£ · 0 0	☐
34 **Loss to be carried back to previous years and set off against income (or capital gains)**	37 **If you're exempt from paying Class 4 NICs, put 'X' in the box**
£ · 0 0	☐
35 **Total loss to carry forward after all other set-offs** – including unused losses brought forward	38 **Total Construction Industry Scheme (CIS) deductions taken from your payments by contractors** – CIS subcontractors only
£ · 0 0	£ · 0 0

HM Revenue & Customs

UK property
Tax year 6 April 2022 to 5 April 2023 (2022–23)

Your name

LUCY FARRINER

Your Unique Taxpayer Reference (UTR)

3 8 7 2 3   7 5 4 0 3

For help filling in this form go to www.gov.uk/taxreturnforms and read the notes and helpsheets.

UK property details

1 Number of properties rented out   2

2 If all property income ceased in 2022–23 and you do not expect to receive such income in 2023–24, put 'X' in the box and consider if you need to fill in the 'Capital Gains Tax summary' page

3 If you have any income from property let jointly, put 'X' in the box

4 If you're claiming Rent a Room relief and your rents are £7,500 or less (or £3,750 if let jointly), put 'X' in the box

Furnished holiday lettings (FHL) in the UK or European Economic Area (EEA)

You need to fill in one page for UK businesses and a separate page for EEA businesses. Read the notes.

5 Income – the amount of rent and any income for services provided to tenants

£   . 0 0

5.1 Property income allowance – read the notes

£   . 0 0

5.2 If you've used traditional accounting rather than cash basis to calculate your income and expenses, put 'X' in the box

6 Rent paid, repairs, insurance and costs of services provided – the total amount

£   . 0 0

7 Loan interest and other financial costs

£   . 0 0

8 Legal, management and other professional fees

£   . 0 0

9 Other allowable property expenses

£   . 0 0

10 Private use adjustment

£   . 0 0

11 Balancing charges

£   . 0 0

11.1 Electric charge-point allowance

£   . 0 0

11.2 Zero-emission car allowance

£   . 0 0

12 Other capital allowances

£   . 0 0

13 Adjusted profit for the year – use the working sheet in the notes

£   . 0 0

14 Loss brought forward used against this year's profits – read the notes if you have a non-FHL property business loss

£   . 0 0

15 Taxable profit for the year (box 13 minus box 14)

£   . 0 0

16 Loss for the year – use the working sheet in the notes

£   . 0 0

17 Total loss to carry forward

£   . 0 0

18 If this business is in the EEA, put 'X' in the box

19 If you want to make a period of grace election, put 'X' in the box

Property income

Do not include furnished holiday lettings, Real Estate Investment Trust or Property Authorised Investment Funds dividends/distributions here.

20 Total rents and other income from property
£ 3 3 4 8 0 . 0 0

21 Tax taken off any income in box 20
£ . 0 0

20.1 Property income allowance – read the notes
£ . 0 0

22 Premiums for the grant of a lease – from box E on the working sheet
£ . 0 0

20.2 If you've used traditional accounting rather than cash basis to calculate your income and expenses, put 'X' in the box

23 Reverse premiums and inducements
£ . 0 0

Property expenses

24 Rent, rates, insurance and ground rents
£ 8 4 7 . 0 0

27 Legal, management and other professional fees
£ . 0 0

25 Property repairs and maintenance
£ 2 1 5 2 . 0 0

28 Costs of services provided, including wages
£ . 0 0

26 Non-residential property finance costs
£ . 0 0

29 Other allowable property expenses
£ . 0 0

Calculating your taxable profit or loss

30 Private use adjustment
£ . 0 0

37 Rent a Room exempt amount
£ . 0 0

31 Balancing charges
£ . 0 0

38 Adjusted profit for the year – use the working sheet in the notes
£ 3 0 4 8 ↑ 0 0

32 Annual Investment Allowance
£ . 0 0

39 Loss brought forward used against this year's profits
£ . 0 0

33 The Structures and Buildings Allowance
£ . 0 0

40 Taxable profit for the year (box 38 minus box 39)
£ 3 0 4 8 ↑ 0 0

33.1 Electric charge-point allowance
£ . 0 0

41 Adjusted loss for the year – use the working sheet in the notes
£ . 0 0

33.2 Freeport Structures and Buildings Allowance
£ . 0 0

42 Loss set off against 2022–23 total income – this will be unusual
£ . 0 0

34 Zero-emission goods vehicle allowance
£ . 0 0

34.1 Zero-emission car allowance
£ . 0 0

43 Loss to carry forward to following year, including unused losses brought forward
£ . 0 0

35 All other capital allowances
£ . 0 0

44 Residential property finance costs
£ . 0 0

36 Costs of replacing domestic items – for residential lettings only
£ . 0 0

45 Unused residential property finance costs brought forward
£ . 0 0

Chapter 7: Business & Financial Goals

Whether you're providing a service with your unique skill set or selling products that you're passionate about, setting clear financial goals is the cornerstone of a thriving business. As a sole trader, your journey is uniquely your own, and so too will be your financial objectives and the paths you choose to achieve them. This chapter is dedicated to helping you articulate what success looks like for you, mapping out your financial targets, and then crafting a strategy that aligns with your business model, whether it's service-based, product-driven, or a hybrid of both.

We will explore the importance of setting goals that not only reflect your aspirations but are also grounded in the reality of your business operations. From the extra cash for life's little luxuries to grand ambitions like property investment or significant business expansion, every goal has its place and purpose. And with every goal comes a tailored strategy – what works for a home-based consultancy won't be the same for a bustling e-commerce platform or a local artisan selling handcrafted goods at markets.

Setting financial goals isn't just about the end result; it's about maintaining focus, staying disciplined in your efforts, and enjoying the satisfaction that comes with each milestone reached. I'll introduce you to tools and resources that can aid your journey, and we'll discuss how to maintain flexibility in your approach, allowing for adjustments as your business and the market evolve.

Financial goals are more than just figures on a financial statement (or tax return!) – they represent the essence of your business vision. Let's refine that vision and set you on a path to achieving the success you envision.

This chapter is split into two parts. First we'll **create** your financial goals, then we'll work out how to **achieve** them. Let's get started!

Harnessing SMARTER Goals for Business Success

Setting goals is a universal imperative for success in any business, and the SMARTER framework provides a robust structure for creating objectives that are not just dreams but achievable targets. SMARTER stands for Specific, Measurable, Achievable, Relevant, Time-bound, Evaluated, and Reflected upon.

By working to these principles, you can create goals that move you forward with purpose and clarity. Let's examine how this works in practice:

Specific
Start by answering the critical "W" questions to define your goal with precision:
- **What** do I want to accomplish with my business?
- **Why** is this goal significant to my personal and business growth?
- **Who** needs to be involved to make this goal a reality?
- **Where** will this endeavour take place? Online, local markets, different geographies?
- **Which** resources, tools, or systems are required?

Measurable

When it comes to setting financial goals for your business, "measurability" is a key factor that gives life to your objectives. It's not just about having an endpoint; it's about being able to track your progress towards that endpoint. The adage by Peter Drucker (my favourite management guru), "What gets measured, gets managed," underscores the power of metrics. It tells us that without measurable outcomes, it's challenging to manage your business's success effectively.

Consider a goal to generate a certain profit margin. If your target is to achieve £1000 in profit each month, and you understand your commission rate or profit on selling your product is 25%, you've already created a clear measure – your business needs to generate £4000 in sales. For service-based businesses, you'll likely have slightly different % rates as much of what goes into your 'product' is your time, so you might have a profit margin that looks more like 80%.

But how do you reach that £4000 mark? Here's where strategy plays a vital role, influenced by the measurability of your goals. One path might involve a high number of small transactions. This could work well if you're running promotions and using social media to reach a broad audience quickly. However, while this might give you a quick win, it may not be sustainable or efficient in the long run due to the constant need to attract new customers.

Alternatively, focusing on building a smaller but more engaged customer base, where the average order value is higher, can be more sustainable. For example, if you create a community, say on Facebook, that regularly interacts with and values your content, you may find that each member's average spend is higher. This doesn't just reduce the number of individual transactions you need to manage, but it also builds a loyal customer base that could provide more consistent revenue.

By shifting the focus to increasing the average order value, you're aiming for quality over quantity, which can improve the customer experience and potentially lead to more referrals. It's a strategy that can help you achieve the same profit goal, but with potentially more significant long-term benefits.

In practice, measuring your progress could involve keeping a close eye on metrics such as:
- **Average order value:** Aiming to increase the average spend of each customer.
- **Customer acquisition cost:** Monitoring how much it costs you to find a new customer and striving to optimise this.
- **Repeat customer rates:** Keeping track of how often customers return to purchase again.
- **Profit margin:** Regularly review your profit margins to ensure they align with your goals.

By specifying these measurable elements, you can fine-tune your business activities and focus on what truly drives your business forward. It's not just about hitting a sales target but doing so in a way that is sustainable and builds a solid foundation for future growth. Remember, every metric you choose to measure and manage should align closely with your overall business strategy and goals.

Achievable

Setting goals that are within your reach is not about scaling down your dreams but rather ensuring that you have the means and strategies in place to realise them. Achievable goals are those that consider your resources, time, and capabilities, ensuring that your ambitions are matched with your current situation and potential for growth.

When you're running your own business, whether it's a consultancy, a craft shop, or a digital marketing agency, it's imperative to align your goals with the time you can invest. For instance, if you're juggling other responsibilities and can dedicate 20 hours a week to your business, your goals need to reflect that. Setting a target that requires a full-time commitment may lead to burnout or disappointment.

A common pitfall in goal setting is to target outcomes that depend on actions from *others*. Instead, aim for goals centred around *your* efforts. For example, rather than setting a goal to "close deals with 10 new clients this month," which hinges on clients' decisions, focus on "initiating conversations with 20 qualified leads this month." This keeps the emphasis on activities within your control.

By setting achievable goals, you're not limiting your business's potential but are strategically setting yourself up for success. It's about making promises to yourself that you can keep, building momentum with each accomplishment, and scaling your aspirations as your business grows.

Relevant
In the pursuit of financial success, setting goals that are relevant to your personal and business trajectory is critical. Relevance in goal-setting ensures that each of your objectives is a building block to your ultimate vision, creating synergy between your immediate actions and your long-term aspirations.

Goals can span various timeframes; some are immediate (short-term), others are set for a little further down the road (medium-term), and some are your distant dreams (long-term). The trick is to ensure these are not at odds with one another.

For example, if you're a freelance graphic designer with a medium-term goal to consistently earn £1500 after tax per month, it's vital that your short-term goals support this. This could include taking on a certain number of projects each month or dedicating time each week to professional development to expand your service offerings.

Your personal life influences your capacity to meet your business goals. If you're planning significant life changes, like starting a family, it's essential to consider how this will impact your ability to work and the time you can dedicate to your business. Conversely, suppose your long-term goal is to secure financial stability to purchase a home. In that case, your business goals should be stepping stones toward accumulating the necessary savings or income to make that happen.

By ensuring each goal supports the next, you're creating a coherent strategy where personal and professional objectives are not just aligned but are actively working in tandem to propel you toward that ultimate milestone.

Time-Bound

Assigning a deadline to your goals is a critical step in the goal-setting process. A time-bound goal anchors your objective within a specific timeframe, significantly enhancing your focus and commitment. By when do you want to achieve your goal? Next month? By the end of the quarter? In two years? Having a clear deadline creates a sense of urgency that can spur you into action.

Why Deadlines Matter:

1. Creates Urgency: Without a deadline, goals can be perpetually postponed. A specific date encourages you to organise your efforts and prioritise tasks.

2. Facilitates Planning: Knowing your deadline helps you to work backwards to create a detailed action plan, setting milestones along the way.

3. Enables Tracking: With a timeline in place, you can measure your progress at regular intervals, ensuring you're on track and making adjustments as needed.

4. Increases Motivation: The closer the deadline, the more motivated you typically are to take action. It can be the push you need to move past procrastination.

5. Encourages Time Management: Time-bound goals require you to manage your time effectively, promoting better work habits and productivity.

So, let's say you're a freelance web developer aiming to increase your income; you might set a goal like, "By the 1st of March 2024, I aim to have secured enough project contracts to ensure a steady monthly income of £2500." This specific timeframe not only gives you a clear target to aim for but also enables you to plan your marketing and client engagement strategy effectively.

It's also beneficial to break down larger, long-term goals into smaller, time-bound segments. This approach allows for regular reassessment of your strategies and keeps you agile in response to changes in the market or your business model.

For example, "By the end of Q1, I will have completed three major project milestones, positioning me to reach my annual revenue target."

Remember, time-bound doesn't just refer to the endpoint. It also applies to the milestones along the way. Each milestone achieved is a step closer to your final goal and an opportunity to celebrate and reinvigorate your efforts.

By defining a clear timeline for your goals, you're not just wishing for success; you're planning for it.

Evaluation

Regular evaluation of your business activities is not just a good practice — it's necessary for growth and improvement. This process allows you to assess what's working and what isn't and to pivot accordingly, ensuring that every task you undertake is contributing effectively towards your goals.

Continual assessment of your efforts helps you determine the effectiveness of your strategies. Are your marketing campaigns yielding the desired results? Is the networking event you attended translating into business opportunities? It's about asking the hard questions and being honest with the answers.

If your current approach isn't garnering the results you anticipated, it's time to delve into the 'why'. Analyse the data, gather feedback, and be willing to learn new methods or enhance your skills. For instance, if your online content isn't engaging your audience, investigate whether the issue lies in the content, the platform, or how it's presented. A tweak in your strategy, like diversifying your content or adjusting your posting schedule, could make a significant difference.

Sometimes, despite your best efforts, a particular tactic may not resonate with your audience. It's essential to remain flexible and consider alternative approaches. Switching from a Facebook page to a group, for example, could foster a more interactive community, aligning better with the platform's algorithms and your audience's preferences.

Evaluate your business performance across various metrics such as social media engagement, sales conversion rates, client satisfaction levels, and financial benchmarks. By maintaining a comprehensive journal of your activities and their outcomes, you can see patterns, understand trends, and make informed decisions.

Remember, what works for one business may not work for another. Personalisation is key. Regularly scheduled evaluation, say weekly, allow you to reflect on your achievements and recalibrate your approach. This could be as specific as, "Every Monday, I will analyse my performance metrics to understand which activities are moving me towards my income goal and which are not, adjusting my efforts accordingly."

By committing to a consistent evaluation process, you not only keep your business aligned with your financial goals but also create a culture of continuous improvement and strategic agility.

Reflection

Reflection is an integral part of the goal-setting and achievement process. It's the moment you take stock of your journey, examining the steps you took to reach your goals and considering what could be enhanced. This practice isn't just about basking in the success of goal completion (although you should definitely take a moment to do a victory dance when you achieve a goal!); it is also a vital learning tool that helps you build wisdom for future endeavours.

Often, it's only in looking back that we gain a full understanding of our experiences. Reflecting on your completed goals allows you to see the efficiency of your strategies and the quality of your execution. What obstacles did you encounter, and how did you overcome them? What unexpected situations arose, and how did you adapt? By reviewing the past, you can distil insights that inform your future.

An essential part of reflection is documentation. By writing down your observations, you crystallise your thoughts and solidify your learnings. This practice ensures that valuable insights aren't lost and that the same mistakes are not repeated. Whether it's a journal entry, a blog post, or a formal report, the act of documenting is as much about recording as it is about processing your experiences.

The ultimate goal of reflection is to take the insights you've gathered and apply them moving forward. As you set new goals, draw upon the lessons from previous ones. Maybe you've learned that certain marketing tactics don't work for your audience, or perhaps you've discovered a more efficient way to manage your workflow. These lessons can refine your approach and increase your effectiveness.

"I will schedule time at the end of each month to reflect on the successes and challenges faced. This will be my opportunity to document the lessons learned and to develop strategies that build on what worked well and improve what didn't."

Reflection is not an endpoint but rather a springboard into the next cycle of goal-setting. It's a powerful mechanism for growth, ensuring that each achievement serves as a foundation for the next.

Your Turn

I've now created some space in the book here to guide you through your first goal-setting exercise. I've broken each stage down so that you can really go deep on your goal setting. You can't do this part wrong, so write whatever you think is best. When you get to the reflection stage of you will be able to review your goal and see whether you could have done it differently. You'll learn by doing, so get stuck in!

Specific
(what, why, who, where, which)

_____
_____
_____
_____
_____
_____
_____

Measurable
(what gets measured gets managed)

_____
_____
_____
_____
_____
_____
_____

Achievable
(do you have the resources and ability)

_____
_____
_____
_____
_____
_____
_____

Relevant
(goal congruence)

_____
_____
_____
_____
_____
_____
_____

Timely
(set yourself a deadline)

_____
_____
_____
_____
_____
_____
_____

Evaluate
(constant evaluation)

_____
_____
_____
_____
_____
_____
_____

Reflect
(take time to inspect your hindsight for any lessons)

_____
_____
_____
_____
_____
_____

Conclude
(write all the parts of your goal together)

_____
_____
_____
_____
_____

_____
_____
_____
_____
_____
_____
_____
_____
_____
_____
_____
_____
_____
_____
_____
_____
_____
_____
_____
_____
_____
_____
_____

How to achieve your financial goals

The second part is to create a plan to **achieve** the goals we have just created.
And it goes like this:

Goals
Reality
Options
Way forward
Tactics
Habit

Goals

We've already worked on creating your goals in the previous section – if you haven't done that yet, I'd advise going back and working on your goals before getting started on this section. If you have your own goals in your head while you read this section, it will set your brain working on what is relevant to you and your goals.

Reality

Reality is about establishing where you are right now in relation to your goal. So if your goal is about bringing in 3 new clients per month, and your current reality is that you are bringing in clients each month, but not in any kind of consistent manner, then you'll need to create a system to bring in clients, ideally a repeatable system. But if you already have a system which is bringing you in 3 clients a month, and your goal is to increase that to 6 clients a month, then your approach in the next part of this process will be different. It's important to realistically evaluate where you are now in order to come up with a good plan to get you where you want to be.

Options

We want to see what options we have that will help us achieve our goals, and this is a two-step process. The first step is to brain-dump all the options you can think of on how you could build your business and achieve your goals. We are not looking for practical reasons not to write an idea down, we are allowing our brain to be creative.   Even if it sounds like a silly idea – write it down.

Let's pretend we are a home-based jewellery maker and we want to sell £2,500 worth of jewellery each month. Let's brainstorm options on how to achieve that:

1. Start an Etsy shop to reach a broader audience, or Amazon or eBay
2. Use Instagram and Pinterest for visual marketing
3. Learn about SEO to better optimise the online store
4. Partner with some local boutiques to feature some of the jewellery we made
5. Create a referral system for existing customers
6. Launch a loyalty program to encourage repeat purchases
7. Introduce a new budget-friendly like for cost-conscious buyer
8. Launch a premium, limited-edition collection
9. Develop a customisable line where customers could choose certain aspects
10. Seasonal promotions or flash sales
11. Start a blog
12. Host a virtual launch party for new collections
13. Offer a cleaning or repair service
14. Launch a subscription box
15. Create a viral dance challenge where participants have to wear our jewellery
16. Write a book about jewellery-making
17. Teach others how to make jewellery through an online course
18. Run workshops to help people make their own jewellery
19. Go to trade shows and networking events to build relationships with suppliers and other crafts people.
20. Start a new trend where pets wear matching owner and pet bracelets
21. Encourage unboxing videos by customers
22. Wholesale deals or consignment arrangements with high-street shops

Can you think of anything else?

_____
_____
_____
_____
_____
_____
_____
_____

_____
_____
_____
_____

Now that we've got all the ideas out, we can look at what our strengths and weaknesses are so that we can see which of our brainstormed options might actually have some legs.

Let's create a profile for a person so that we can identify their strengths and weaknesses:

Isabella is a creative and passionate individual who has turned her love for jewellery-making into a small business. She works from her home studio, where she designs and crafts each piece by hand. Isabella has a background in arts and has taken several courses in jewellery-making. She's in her mid-30s, detail-oriented, patient, and has a good eye for trends. Isabella sells her creations at local craft fairs and through her online store. She is a one-woman show, managing everything from production to sales, and she prides herself on the personal touch she adds to all her customer interactions.

STRENGTHS	WEAKNESSES
⇒ With my artistic background, I have ability to create unique and appealing designs.	⇒ My time management isn't very good, I get overwhelmed by everything I have to do to run a business.
⇒ I am meticulous in my attention to detail, so my jewellery is always made to a high standard.	⇒ I have no clue about finances, I'm not even sure if I'm making a profit.
⇒ I have an innate sense for current and upcoming fashion trends.	⇒ Social media baffles me – what should I be posting about on social media?!
⇒ I am very personable which allows me to build strong relationships.	⇒ I'm so passionate about what I do, I'm scared to involve anyone else in case they

Way Forward

At this stage, we look at the different options we have and decide which will be the best/fastest/cheapest/most likely to succeed based on what our strengths and weaknesses are.

Depending on the type of person you are, a simple pros & cons list might be the best way to decide.
Or go with your heart; one option will seem exciting and motivating, while another will make you feel tired before you even start.

Option 1 – Run a workshop to help people make their own jewellery

<u>Pros</u>
- ⇒ Strengthens my brand as an educator in the field rather than just a seller
- ⇒ Creates a new channel for showcasing my expertise and creativity
- ⇒ Develops deeper connections with customers who might become brand advocates
- ⇒ Offers a platform for personalised customer interactions, enhancing loyalty
- ⇒ Provides an additional revenue stream
- ⇒ Workshops can generate word of mouth referrals
- ⇒ Opportunity to capture content for social media

<u>Cons</u>
- ⇒ Hosting workshops could be time-consuming – how much jewellery could I make in the time I spend organising, prepping and running the workshop?
- ⇒ Do I have the skills or patience to run events like that?
- ⇒ Risks regarding setting up a workshop and then no-one coming
- ⇒ Will I spread myself too thin leading to burnout?
- ⇒ This will reduce the time I have to innovate and design new pieces which could stifle my creativity.

One person reading this might say it's a no-brainer, absolutely run the workshop, the pros far outweigh the cons, do it! Another person might look at this and say oh my goodness, there's so much risk there, it's not worth it at all. The answer to whether or not this is a way forward for you and your business is completely dependent on who you are – your risk profile, your interests and your passions.

Tactics

The way forward is the big picture, strategy – the direction you will go with your business. Tactics is more about creating a step by step plan to make that happen. This part will also help with your reflections at the end; if you have written down your step by step guide, you can use it as an aide-memoire to help you identify any weak areas of your process.

Let's have a look at what Isabella's tactics might be for her to run a workshop:

- ☐ Design the curriculum for the workshop
- ☐ Prepare the materials – supplies and what participants will take home
- ☐ Do a trial run of the workshop to estimate how long it will take
- ☐ Teach the process to my sister to see if she understands how I'm teaching it
- ☐ Ask my accountant to sit with me for half an hour to work out the costs and what I should sell tickets for
- ☐ Design the images to market the workshop on social media
- ☐ Create an event on Facebook and ask people to share it
- ☐ Design and put up flyers on local craft stores, coffee shops and community boards
- ☐ Partner with local businesses for cross-promotion

☐ List the workshop on local event websites and craft forums

☐ Share behind-the-scenes preparations on social media to build interest

Isabella might want to break these down into tasks to make them more manageable as she goes through it.

Habits

Any part of your plan that involves repetitive actions will be MUCH more manageable if you create a habit around doing it.

For example, if you plan to post to your Facebook group twice every day, then choose an activity that you do twice a day that will act as a trigger to remind you to post. For example, it could be brushing your teeth; when you brush your teeth, it reminds you to go and open your laptop and post something interesting to your group. Or, if you've already pre-prepared your images, you could sit on the toilet after you've done your teeth (with the lid down…I'm not suggesting anything else…although you can if you want!!) and post from your phone.

Look back at your tactics plan and see what repetitive items you could create a habit around.

My Achieving Worksheet

Goals
(reminder)

_____
_____
_____
_____
_____
_____
_____
_____
_____
_____
_____
_____
_____
_____
_____
_____
_____
_____
_____
_____
_____
_____
_____
_____
_____

Reality
(what is your current situation in relation to your goal?)

_____
_____
_____
_____
_____
_____
_____
_____
_____
_____
_____
_____
_____
_____
_____
_____
_____
_____

Options
(Brainstorm all the ideas, then write your strength and weaknesses)

_____
_____
_____
_____
_____
_____
_____
_____
_____
_____
_____
_____
_____
_____
_____
_____
_____
_____
_____
_____
_____
_____
_____

STRENGTHS	WEAKNESSES

Way forward
(best of your options)

_____
_____
_____
_____
_____
_____
_____
_____
_____
_____

Tactics
(detailed task list following your Way Forward)

_____
_____
_____
_____
_____
_____
_____
_____
_____
_____
_____
_____
_____
_____
_____
_____
_____
_____
_____
_____
_____
_____
_____
_____

Habits
(what repetitive actions could you create habits out of?)

_____
_____
_____
_____
_____
_____
_____
_____
_____
_____
_____
_____
_____
_____
_____
_____
_____
_____
_____
_____
_____
_____
_____

Any Other Thoughts

_____
_____
_____
_____
_____
_____
_____
_____
_____
_____
_____
_____
_____
_____
_____
_____
_____

How to Develop a Prosperity Mindset

Having a prosperity mindset is a crucial factor in reaching your financial goals. It keeps you on track toward your goals regardless of any challenges you encounter. These strategies below will help you foster a prosperity mindset that can enable you to live the life you desire.

Keep Your Focus
If you find that your mind wanders from idea to idea, create one set plan and stick to it. In your plan, make a list of specific achievable action steps that lead to your goal, and then work on at least one task each day to help maintain your focus.

Plan for Success
It doesn't matter how focused you are if you don't have a proper plan. Your financial goals will not happen just by deciding on a number. Instead, make some clear plans on how you're going to get there – all you need to do is follow the instructions in the previous section. This will get you past the *dream phase* to start making your ultimate goals a reality.

Be as detailed in your plan as possible, and set each task as a mini-goal. Achieving these small goals every day keeps you motivated and moving toward your big goal.

Model Yourself After Successful People
One of the best decisions you can make is to use other successful people as your role models. First, think about what you admire about these people and then try to model their behaviour.

You will also want to study the reasons why they've become successful. How do you think they got to where they are? Can you embark on a similar journey? The chances are that you can; all you need to do is build up the courage to achieve.

Believe in Yourself
 Unfortunately, too many people don't have confidence in their abilities. As a result, they fail to try or give up far too quickly. You don't have to be one of these people!

Look back at the people you admire, and you'll likely notice that they felt like giving up at some point. But they didn't! They probably have an unwavering belief in their abilities and a drive to succeed, no matter what.

You *can* reach your financial goals! Believe that it *is* possible! People have proven that it's possible and ***you can achieve anything possible.***

Pay It Forward
 Along your journey to success, you can practise good karma by paying it forward. Spread your knowledge so that others can learn the lessons you've learned. You can serve as a mentor to others just like you were mentored when starting.

When you are kind to others, that kindness will find its way right back to you. You never know what good can come out of some simple kindness.

Developing your prosperity mindset may take some time and effort, but the rewards are well worth it. Once you've mastered it, it will be with you for the rest of your life, guiding you to achieve any financial goals you desire.

Chapter 8: Productivity & Time Management

Do you ever procrastinate? Would you like to put a stop to this time-wasting habit? You can make progress today by breaking your to-do list into mini-tasks.

A mini-task is a task that is so small you couldn't make it any smaller without being silly about it. Posting on an Avon Facebook Group to ask a specific question would be a good example of a mini-task.

In general, mini-tasks take 15 minutes or less to accomplish.

This time management technique addresses one of the most common causes of procrastination on larger projects: uncertainty about where to get started. For example, writing a book is a sequence of achievable tasks, but people frequently have a difficult time even getting started on such a seemingly huge project.

Ideally, you would plan the entire process from beginning to end. This may not always be possible; some projects have too much uncertainty to be able to predict the entire process from the beginning. But you could still develop a task list for as far as you are able to see. At some point, you'll be able to see further down the path and can develop new mini-tasks.

Let's use a simple example: Setting up your Facebook Page for Customers. I've filled this out a bit with more info on the marketing side as I know this will be helpful for some people!

My Task List – Setting up my Facebook Page

☐ Decide who my ideal customer will be
Maybe you decide you want to focus on people who want to buy perfume.

☐ Write up my Avatar to deep dive into my ideal customer.
Who they are, where they hang out etc. There are plenty of exercises around to take you through creating an Avatar step by step if you Google it

☐ Create an image for my profile picture
Make sure it shows your face and would appeal to your ideal customer. Canva is a great product to use for this.

☐ Create a cover image for my page.
Make sure it shows the personality of your business, and even if you use it to showcase a different offer every month, try to keep the basic look the same so that people recognise it when they come to your page.

☐ Create a posting schedule for the next social media campaign.
Don't just plan sales posts... look at what other pages to do to increase engagement and adapt that to work for you and your audience.

☐ Create some content to post for now.
When you share your page, it will need to have some content on it.

☐ Update my profile to show your page.
People on Facebook are nosy; they will visit your profile to see who you are and what you do. If you don't have your page on your profile, you may be missing out on new customers as they will click through to your page if they are interested.

☐ Share my page.
Share your page to your profile and ask anyone who is interested to like your page – make it clear that you're not asking for anyone and everyone to like it; please only people who are interested in what you're sharing. The Facebook algorithm won't work if you just have lots of likes from people who aren't interested and won't engage; it will hurt you more than help you.

Number 5 might still seem like a huge job, so you could break it down even further:

☐ Find a posting schedule download from the internet.

☐ Look at 3 of my favourite pages to see the type of things they post and what gets the most engagement. Write notes about the themes that I notice.

☐ Fill in my plan for the next campaign.

☐ Create 3 new posts on Monday and schedule to post on Monday, Tuesday and Wednesday at 6 pm.

☐ Create 3 new posts on Tuesday and schedule to post on Thursday, Friday and Saturday at 6 pm.
And so on.

A good rule of thumb is that if the thought of completing the task fills you with dread, you might feel less daunted if you break your process down into smaller tasks.

More Benefits of Mini-Task Lists

A list of mini-tasks is like a recipe; all you have to do is move down the list. When you get to the end, you're done. *None of the tasks should take a lot of time or be so complex that you're hesitant to complete the step.*

An added benefit of making such a list is that you'll have an excellent idea of how long the overall project will take. Assigning an accurate time estimate without having really considered all the tasks involved can feel challenging.

Making a list of mini-tasks can also be an effective way to plan your day. Even if you don't think this will work for you, give it a try for a few days and see.

The evening before, make a list of all the tasks you need to do for the following day. This likely means a list of 50 or so items. This might very well be overkill but try it anyway. You can always scale back as needed. If you often feel like you never get anything done, this might be a great tool to apply daily.

Mini-tasks are a viable way of completing large or complex projects.

By breaking everything down into simple, small, and manageable components, you are much less likely to procrastinate. For a lot of people, this is a very effective way to consistently get a lot done. Try mini-tasking instead of multi-tasking and watch your efficiency soar!

Do More in Less Time - And Have More Time for Yourself

Getting things done brings such a great feeling of accomplishment, but it can also be overwhelming if the task seems insurmountable. Sometimes the days just don't seem long enough to do everything we want to do. When that happens worry can set in, but it doesn't have to!

You can do more than you ever thought was possible, and in less time too, giving yourself time to relax and really enjoy life!

It all begins with a solid foundation of time management and scheduling. It's okay if you're not a good time manager right now, you can learn to be. It just takes a little bit of practice and you'll soon be getting more and more done.

When you see how much you are accomplishing, you'll work even harder during your busy times, and enjoy those down times more thoroughly.

These scheduling strategies will help you become an expert manager of your time:

Schedule your life for maximum benefit. You can avoid procrastination and the big stressed-out rush to meet a deadline by scheduling each day and using just a bit of self-discipline to stick to your schedule.

By scheduling your day according to your priorities, you can better utilise the time that you might otherwise have wasted doing unproductive things, like watching television or waiting for the next item on your to-do list to come to you.

Disallow doubts from getting in your way. That little voice in the back of your mind that tells you, *"It's too much work,"* or *"It's not going to happen,"* does not know what it is talking about!

You can do anything you set your mind to. Keep that thought in mind as you go through your day. The more you think it - or even say it out loud - the more you'll internalise and believe it.

When you remind yourself how much you are capable of doing, you'll work harder so you can reap the rewards of being done with work.

No matter how you reward yourself, make it a point to do so regularly. Finished that presentation? Take the evening off and watch your favourite movie! Whatever reward works for you is a good one - as long as the work is done first.

Recognise when you're getting stressed and why. Sometimes in an effort to get more done, you'll find that you aren't getting the time for yourself that you'd hoped for. When this happens, stop and reassess your schedule.

Are you following your agenda? Are you productive during your scheduled working times? Are you meeting your goals? Where can you make changes for better success?

Do you concentrate and get your work done during your working hours? If not, you may find that you still have to work when you should be relaxing. This is a vicious circle that leaves you feeling stressed, while getting nowhere.

Eliminate your stressors while building in stress relief. Think about the following as you go about your workday:

By focusing during working hours, you'll complete each task much sooner. Get your drudgery tasks out of the way as quickly as possible to make more time for more enjoyable tasks.

Work time is for work only - so avoid distractions. Ringing phones and other issues can stop you from accomplishing your work. Forward calls to your voice mail and establish "do not disturb" times. You'll be amazed at how much work you can get done without distractions!

If you complete your tasks early, keep working until your schedule says it's time to stop. Perhaps you can tackle some work for the next day to get ahead. Being a little ahead gives you the flexibility to take care of inevitable emergencies without falling behind in productivity.

Recognise when you need a break. People are not machines so your schedule should reflect that. Realistic break times should be part of even the busiest schedule.

By planning your time wisely, you will accomplish more and be able to reap the many benefits of true relaxation when you're done. It's well worth the effort!

Each Step I Take Leads to the Life That I Want

Chapter 9: Marketing Your Business

In this new age of online opportunity, there are many ways of selling your products and services without even having to leave your house. All you need is an internet connection and a computer or device that allows you access to the internet.

Let's have a deeper look into different aspects of marketing that you could use to help you find more customers and clients for your business.

Self-Branding

Every sole trader should be aware of self-branding. Self-branding is marketing yourself. It's important to market everything associated with your business, and that includes you. Many people will buy from you because of who you are and not just because of what you're offering. If this wasn't true, most people would just go to the website and order direct.

It's a well-known fact that people buy from those they know, like, and trust. Even if a prospect is excited about what your product can do for him, much of his decision is about you. So let's see how you can get your lovely face out front and centre.

Create your image
It's not just about putting your name and face on everything you do. You need to decide on what image you want to present. It should truly be you, but it should focus on integrity and your strengths. How do you want potential customers to view you?

Your image should be represented by everything you say and do in your marketing materials. That includes every email you send out and every conversation you have. Keep that image constant.

Give this some serious thought. Consider the type of person with whom you would want to do business. That's the type of person you want to be. That's the image you want others to have of you.

Get yourself noticed
Whenever you're marketing Avon products, include yourself in the marketing. The two are forever entwined.

Send out regular updates to all your customers and leads. Tell them what you're doing and what's going on. If they like you, they're more likely to purchase from you. Give them a reason to like you.

Write relevant articles and post them online. Then, send links to those articles to the same people.

Attend industry events whenever you can. Shake some hands. Give a talk. Pass out flyers. Make some friends. Do everything you can without being a pest.

Become an expert
For example, become known as the expert on building an email list or on building a great downline, or if you want to focus on being a rep without becoming a sales leader, become an expert on different make-up or hair styles using Avon products. It's easier to become an expert on one thing than on ten. The

funny thing is, once you're considered to be an expert on one aspect of Avon, you're assumed to be an expert on everything related to Avon.

Being considered an expert carries a lot of power. There is no better way to boost your self-brand.

Be part of your community
Get out in your community and spread the good word (tactfully) about how great you and your business really are. It's not just about marketing your products; it's about marketing yourself, too. Give your image a lot of thought; it really is critical to your success.
When your self-brand improves, so do your sales, and your business grows as a result!

Volunteer
Join your local chamber of commerce. Find something worthwhile to be part of and contribute your time. Not only are you being a good person, but you're also getting your brand out there in a very positive way. This makes for great material to put on your web page or your email updates.

Conclusion
If you can't sell yourself, it's very difficult to sell your products. So work on your self-branding and make it part of your life. Consider every interaction you have, to be an opportunity to present yourself in a way that is consistent with the image you want to project.

Marketing on Facebook

Facebook Page or Facebook Group?
What is the difference?! A page is basically a shop window, you can share information, yes people can comment on it, but it's more of a broadcast platform. A group is much more intimate and all about the engagement. If you're looking to form relationships, do it in a group.

A group can be setup as either public or private, so either everyone can see all the posts and comments, regardless of whether they are a member of the group or not, whereas a private group will only allow you to see the posts and comments if you are a member.

Boosting Posts or Paid Ads
For the most part, you should avoid boosted posts. Yes, you might get a little more engagement on the post, but will it result directly in more sales? Unless you are logging all your views and engagement and see a definitely up

Marketing on Instagram

What started as a mobile app to share photos has evolved into a diverse social media platform.

With over 1 billion users - about 60% of whom use the app daily - Instagram is the perfect platform to grow your audience and build brand awareness. In fact, 83% of users have said they discovered new products or services via Instagram.

Follow these tips to get started on Instagram:

Create account

With a Business or Creator account, you have access to additional insights, analytics, ability to advertise and special profile benefits (such as contact info).

Optimise

Take the steps to optimise your profile so people can easily find you in search and learn about your business by looking at your profile.

- Use a recognisable profile picture
- Have searchable username and name
- Choose the correct category for your business
- Write an engaging, descriptive bio
- Include website and contact information
-

Hashtags

Hashtags help categorise your content. You can use up to 30 hashtags per post. Choose at least one relevant hashtag so that users can find your business.

Types of Post

There are a variety of ways you can share content and engage your audience on Instagram:

- **Grid.** Your grid displays photos and videos that appear on your profile. Your posts can have captions with up to 2,200 characters. Keep in mind that the first two lines of your caption will appear before a "Read More" prompt. With this in mind, write the first two lines to be engaging or incite curiosity.

- **Stories**. Stories are photos or videos that disappear after 24 hours unless they are added to your profile highlights. You can post more often. More behind the scenes.

- **IGTV.** You can post vertical, longer form videos via Instagram's IGTV platform. These IGTV videos can also be displayed on your grid and stories.

- **Reels.** Instagram Reels are 15-30 second vertical video clips that can be shared on your stories as well. These are a great way to engage your current audience.

From there, you can create a content schedule of what to post on Instagram.

Types of Content to Post on Social Media

The main focus you need to have, whether you're posting on Instagram, Facebook Pages or Groups or any other social media platform, is about engagement. The more engagement your post gets, the more the algorithms on the respective platforms with circulate your content with other people. The more you're seen, the more potential customers you'll find.

Behind-the-scenes
Post content that shows followers the behind-the-scenes of your business.

Motivational
Curate shareable, inspirational quotes that align with your brand values and resonate with your audience. Add your company's branding to quote graphics you post on social media!

Tutorial
Tutorials and how-to's guide your customers through specific problems. Tutorials are great targeted marketing examples because you know prospects who land on a tutorial are there to solve a specific problem.

Video
There are a number of ways you can add video to Instagram, including Instagram stories, 60-second grid videos, 15-30 second reels, or on IGTV.

User-Generated Content
Sharing posts from your followers can be a great way to build a relationship with those followers, engage with other followers, and effortlessly fill your content schedule!

Case studies and testimonials
This type of content uses real stories to show followers about your product or service. Through real customer stories, you can show that you understand customer pain points.

Storytelling
This type of content tells your brand's story. Even though it's a story, there should be a lesson here. Storytelling content builds awareness and engages your prospective customers.

By balancing between these types of content, you hit many goals, including expanding your reach, connecting with your customer, and telling them about your business.

There are plenty of ways to grow your reach and market on Instagram. It's a dynamic platform that gives you many ways to connect with viewers and humanize your brand!

Email Marketing

Despite what you may have heard, email marketing is still one of the best ways to market online.

The first step is to build an email list. Offer something valuable, such as a free report or discount coupon, that is related to your products or services in exchange for their email address.

To run a successful email marketing campaign, it's important to understand your audience and what they want. Once you understand what they want, you can craft an offer that will be attractive to them and then make your offer in an email to your list.

Autoresponders

To build your email list and send emails to them, you'll need to use an autoresponder. This software also allows you to track the effectiveness of your emails – so if you are not getting much response from certain types of emails or when they are sent at certain times of day, you'll know you need to adjust your approach.

When it comes to choosing one and using it, my advice would be just to pick one and start using it. All the major autoresponder platforms have numerous guides and articles about how to use them to run successful marketing campaigns.

I highly recommend Mail Chimp – there's a free first-level subscription, so you can test the waters without paying anything, and it's also fairly user-friendly. If you start becoming (or plan to become!) a bigger user with bigger lists, it would be worth spending the time now doing your shopping around the options before settling.

You can find loads of videos on YouTube that teach how to run email marketing campaigns with your chosen autoresponder and video reviews of the different platforms if you're having a hard time trying to choose.

Building an email list

Once you have got to grips with how to use the software, the next thing you need to look at is building an email list.

If people are visiting your website, chances are good that they are interested in what you have to offer. Make a form available for them to join your email list and be kept in the loop about future product releases or special offers. And share that page to social media – if you don't have a website, you can share signup forms directly from within Mail Chimp.

Once they've signed up to this email list, you can send emails to these prospects with news and further information about your products. Let them know whenever something goes on special offer.

Email marketing is one of the best ways to drive sales. Treat your list members like gold because that's what they are to you and your business.

Search Engine Marketing

SEM is a major part of online marketing and is split into two defined areas: search engine optimisation and Pay-Per-Click advertising. I'm including this here for completeness, but honestly unless you have the time to really get to know what you're doing in this area, I would focus on the social media platforms that you currently use rather than venturing into a whole new area of the internet!

Search Engine Optimisation (SEO)

With SEO, you'll learn how to optimise a website so that it ranks higher in the search engines' organic results, therefore helping to drive targeted traffic to your website.

An important item to understand about SEO is that this is a discipline that changes continuously. Because of this aspect, you'll want to monitor the major players in SEO to keep up with search engine algorithm changes, so you can adjust your own methods accordingly.

Pay-Per-Click Advertising (PPC)

PPC will enable you to send traffic to websites with targeted advertisements.

Google Ads is still one of the most popular PPC networks, which will show your ads on Google properties and websites that have the AdSense code included.

You can learn PPC easily online and relatively quickly. There are numerous courses you can take, including ones that will allow you to gain a Google Certification for PPC ads.

This chapter is designed to give you a high level introduction to marketing, google things to find out more, ask questions in the Facebook group, join the online monthly meet-ups – use this information as a springboard from which to further understand what it's all about and how you can use it to build your business.

Answers to the Case Studies in Chapter 3

Case Study: Creative Designs by Mia

In Mia's case, claiming a holiday as a business expense would likely be incorrect according to standard tax guidelines. For an expense to be allowable, it must be wholly and exclusively for the purpose of the business. While Mia may feel inspired and come up with new ideas during her holiday, the primary purpose of the trip is personal relaxation and not a direct business activity or need.

The fact that she rationalised the holiday as a reward for hard work and a chance for inspiration suggests that it was not solely for business purposes. Tax authorities typically do not allow holidays to be expensed even if the individual engages in some business activities during the trip. If Mia were to be investigated, she would need to justify the expense, and it's likely that the cost would be disallowed, potentially leading to penalties or additional tax liabilities.

For an expense to be deductible, it would need to have a clear business purpose, such as attending a conference directly related to her field, with documented evidence of attendance and the direct link to her business activities.

Case Study: Liam's Landscaping Services

Liam's decision to claim his daughter's day care fees as a business expense is not typically allowed under tax regulations. Childcare costs, while necessary for Liam to work, are considered personal expenses. The tax authorities generally stipulate that business expenses must be directly related to the running and operation of the business itself. Childcare, though it indirectly enables Liam to focus on his work, does not directly relate to the landscaping services he provides and is not exclusively for the purposes of the business.

For an expense to be deductible, it must be wholly and exclusively for the business. In this case, childcare is a dual-purpose expense, serving the personal need of caring for his child and the indirect benefit of allowing him to work. Consequently, childcare costs are not considered an allowable business expense for tax purposes. Liam should not include these costs in his tax return as business expenses, as doing so could result in a disallowed claim or potential penalties if audited by tax authorities.

Case Study: Elena's Freelance Writing Venture

Elena's approach to claiming expenses in her tax return requires a nuanced understanding of business expenses, capital expenditures, and operational expenses.

Home office furniture and laptop: these items are typically considered capital expenditures rather than immediate business expenses. Capital expenditures are assets that have a useful life beyond the tax year and thus are not necessarily fully deductible in the year of purchase, but instead claimed over a number of years as a capital allowance. As these are items of furniture, it's highly likely they would be fully allowed in the current tax year, but not all assets are, so it's important to check.

Subscriptions to magazines and journals: the subscriptions can be considered operational expenses, as they are regular expenses that directly relate to the running of her freelance writing business. These costs are incurred for the purpose of staying informed and relevant in her field, which is essential for her content creation work. Therefore, claiming the full cost of these subscriptions in her tax return as business expenses is appropriate and aligns with standard practices for

Printed in Great Britain
by Amazon

35131708R00071